The

GOOGLE
RÉSUMÉ

The

GOOGLE
RÉSUMÉ

How to Prepare for a Career
and Land a Job at Apple, Microsoft, Google,
or any Top Tech Company

Gayle Laakmann McDowell

WILEY

John Wiley & Sons, Inc.

Published by John Wiley & Sons, Inc., Hoboken, New Jersey.
Published simultaneously in Canada.

For general information on our other products and services or for technical support, please contact our Customer Care Department within the United States at (800) 762-2974, outside the United States at (317) 572-3993 or fax (317) 572-4002.

Wiley also publishes its books in a variety of electronic formats. Some content that appears in print may not be available in electronic books. For more information about Wiley products, visit our web site at www.wiley.com.

Library of Congress Cataloging-in-Publication Data:

McDowell, Gayle Laakmann, 1982-
   The google résumé : how to prepare for a career and land a job at Apple, Microsoft, Google, or any top tech company / Gayle Laakmann McDowell.
      p. cm.
   Includes index.
   ISBN 978-0-470-92762-5 (hardback)
   ISBN 978-1-118-01313-7 (ebk)
   ISBN 978-1-118-01314-4 (ebk)
   ISBN 978-1-118-01315-1 (ebk)
          1. Résumés (Employment)   2. High technology industries—Vocational guidance.
3. Job hunting. I. Title.
   HF5383.M335   2011
   650.14'2—dc22

                                                                              2010039906

Printed in the United States of America

10 9 8 7 6 5 4 3 2 1

To my mother and grandmother,
whose engineering endeavors paved the way for my own.

Contents

Chapter 1

Introduction

Just so you're clear: it was not my idea to give a talk to Microsoft Research. I had learned embarrassingly little about computer science in my 18 years of life, and the last thing I wanted to do is to have that exposed in front of a bunch of genius PhDs in MSR. But my manager thought it'd be a great "opportunity," and so there I was, blabbing on about my summer project.

I finished up my talk at lightning speed. As I was dealing with a somewhat severe case of stage fright, I considered my haste a good thing. And then the questions started. Did I consider doing X? Yes, I told them, I did, and this is what happened. Why not implement it with Y? You could, but that would cause problem Z.

I almost hesitated to admit it to myself afterwards, but things went fine. Just fine.

That whole summer I had been convinced that Microsoft would discover that I knew practically nothing and cut me loose. I had only gotten my internship offer through some brilliant streak of luck, I reasoned, and didn't really deserve it. Not like my fellow interns did anyway. They had done three times as much college as me, completed three times as many projects, and basically knew three times as much as me.

Four years later, with a job at Google about to start, I reflected on my incredible luck. I landed a Microsoft internship at an incredibly young age, and that turned into three consecutive internships. Then I got an Apple internship, even though Apple never even recruited at my university. And then I happened to get hooked up with just the right people who referred me to the up-and-coming Google. I must be the luckiest person alive.

Or am I?

Maybe, while Lady Luck was certainly in my favor, I had somehow, accidentally, done everything just right. I completed several large projects in high school, offering me considerably more experience than my peers. I got an entry-level job as a web designer, which developed my professional and technical credibility. I created a résumé that, while atrocious in many respects, demonstrated my passion for technology and showcased my limited experience. And finally, I built a network of more senior professionals, managed relationships with mentors, and leveraged these connections to land one dream job after another.

And that, my dear readers, is how you get a job at the world's greatest tech companies.

Life at Infinite Loop and Microsoft Way

Even their addresses are suggestive of company stereotypes. Microsoft, at One Microsoft Way, screams big and mammoth. Google's 1600 Amphitheatre Parkway address is understated, like its user interfaces. Apple, of course, takes the bold "think different" step with One Infinite Loop—a play on words that could come back to bite a less beloved company.

Youthful

Despite the little eccentricities of each company, these companies are much more alike than they are different. Software companies are youthful—at heart, if not in actuality. They scorn the stuffy suits-and-ties atmosphere of their predecessors and elect to wear just jeans and a T-shirt. In fact, this casual attitude is so potent that it's pervaded even the social scenes of tech hubs; only a small handful of restaurants in Seattle and San Francisco would request anything beyond jeans, and a woman in a suit gets more stares than a girl with a purple mohawk.

Perks

Desperate to attract and retain the best and the brightest, tech firms shower their employees with perks. Microsoft offers free drinks, a heavily discounted gym membership, and an all-expenses-paid health care plan. Google matched and then one-upped Microsoft on almost all of these. Free sodas? Try free breakfast, lunch, and dinner. Free gym membership? Use the on-site gym and pool. Deluxe health care plan? We'll give you a good one, and throw in an on-site doctor. Nerds everywhere can only hope that the "next Google," whatever it is, will engage in its own perk war.

Of course, cynics argue that these benefits are really just a way to trick employees into staying at the office longer. You can fulfill almost any regular appointment, from a haircut to dry cleaning, without leaving campus. But the fact that you *can* doesn't mean you have to. No one will think worse of you because you declined to get your dental work done from the on-site dentist parked in the van out back.

Work / Life Balance

The severe shortage of engineers in the United States forces companies to take good care of their employees. They would lose too many qualified candidates otherwise.

Workers are encouraged to find a reasonable work/life balance, and work comparatively short hours compared to people from other industries.

The exception, as in most jobs, is during crunch times. Software releases will be stressful in any team.

Moving Up: Individual Contributors

Although other industries push high-performing employees into management roles, technology companies tend to be more open to the "individual contributor" role. After all, great engineers do not necessarily make the best managers.

An employee, particularly in engineering, can continue to get promotions and increased technical responsibilities, without becoming a people manager. Eventually, this employee can grow into an architect or a distinguished engineer, earning one of the most respected positions within the company. It's perhaps not as glamorous as being a VP, but for some people, this is just right.

The Differences

Cultural differences between companies can often be traced back to the company's roots.

Amazon, many would argue, is more of a retail company than a software company. It faced extremely hard times during the dot-com crash, and continues to battle profit margins that are levels of magnitude lower than that of a "core" software company. It is consequently extremely frugal, and refrains from providing the lavish perks that others software companies might. Additionally, some employees have suggested that the company does not value technical innovation for its own sake, and instead looks for an immediate and causal link to profits. But, do not let that deter you too much; indeed, Amazon is leading in multiple industries (retail, cloud computing, etc.) largely because of its technical innovation. The company moves at a rapid pace and pending deadlines often mean late nights.

Apple is just as secretive inside as it is outside. When your innovation lies so heavily in your look and feel and your market share depends on beautifully orchestrated hype, it's no wonder. The company can't afford to let its secrets slip. Employees are die-hard fans, just as one would expect, but rarely know what coworkers from other teams are working on. In my time at the company, I sensed a feared-but-revered attitude toward Steve Jobs; he called the shots, and no one would argue.

Microsoft has dabbled (and reasonably successfully) with search and the web, but a large chunk of its earnings come from Windows and Office. Live patches to these products are expensive, so the company tends to operate on longer, multiyear release schedules. This means moving slower, taking fewer risks, and making sure to get everything right the first time (even if it's never totally right). The bright side is that the company tends to have a good work/life balance, as ship dates are relatively infrequent. Many former employees say that though they loved the company, its mammoth size could stifle innovation and risk-taking. However, individual team cultures are all over the map, and some may be more innovative than others.

Google is the nerdiest of the nerdy. Founded by two former Stanford PhDs, the company is still, many claim, preferential to engineers over other positions. The company moves quickly, shipping products weekly, and can value technical innovation even to a fault. As a web-based company, it can afford to take some risks on products; after all, "shipping" a new application to the web is so much easier than boxing up and mailing software. Google values its flat hierarchy, but there's a downside as well. Your manager may have too many people under her to fuss about the progress of your career, and moving up can be a challenge.

Big vs. Little: Is a Start-up Right for You?

Go to almost any business school and you'll find that there are about three times as many people who claim to be "interested" in start-ups than actually pursuing this career path. Why? Because start-ups are sexy.

Newspapers splash stories about start-ups that made it big, or crashed and burned, and we always think, *we can do that* or *we can do better*. Start-ups are a high-stakes game, and you're gambling with your time as well as your money.

For the right person with the right opportunity, however, a start-up environment can be fantastic.

The Good

Many say that for true "start-up people," this high-risk career is just in their nature. They get that entrepreneurial itch, either in college or at some big company, and know they need to be somewhere much, much smaller. And their new career path offers a ton of value to them in return:

- **Diversity of skills.** Whereas big companies have designated marketing and finance people, start-ups never have enough people to fill every role. And the smaller the company, the more hats you have to wear. Unless you are truly narrowly focused on just one field (in which case you should avoid start-ups), this can be a great thing. You'll get to develop a more diverse skill set, which will help you in your future job search.

- **Leadership opportunities.** When—or if—your start-up grows, you'll be in a great place to lead your own team. Many people join a company and find that within months they're expected to manage several new hires. You'd have to be at a bigger company for years to get such an opportunity.

- **Control and influence.** Each time a bit of my work shipped at a big company, I was able to point to it and say, "I did that." And while that made me happy, a little part of me also knew that, really, someone else would have come along and done something very similar if I hadn't been there. At a start-up, however, you are not only shaping the company in how you perform your immediate responsibilities, but you're also offering feedback on all aspects of the business. Think the newsletter should have some content about related tools and plug-ins? It's your job to speak up, and everyone will listen. You always know the decision makers in any department.

- **Rapid results.** You won't have to wait years to see your work out in the real world; it'll happen within months. That holds true for any decisions you make as well. For better or worse, the outcome is visible within months, enabling you to learn from your mistakes (and successes) much faster.
- **High reward.** Hey, we don't take on all this risk for nothing. Start-ups can make you very, very rich if you get very lucky. Of course, it could just as well do absolutely nothing for you financially—and usually that's the case.

Me? I'm a start-up person. I love everything about it. I love that I get to do 10 things at once. And if I have no idea how to do it, then I get to learn. I see my impact immediately and I know that, for better or worse, I shaped the company's future.

The Bad

Start-up burnout is a very real thing. Sure, you may be passionate about your new social-location-group-buying-thingy-dot-com, but things change and passions die. The following stresses tend to wear on people the most.

- **Long hours.** With the amount of money and careers depending on a start-up's success, long hours are critical. Those who do the bare minimum don't last long, and start-ups do not have the fear of firing underperformers that bigger companies do.
- **Unclear job description.** You were hired in to be a tester, and now you're helping look for office space. Well, tough. Someone's got to do it. Start-ups don't have the time and money to hire a specialist for each and every task, so employees are

expected to chip in on projects that are outside of their roles. That may mean you spend less time doing what you love and more time doing what the company wants you to do.

- **Low pay.** With very few exceptions, start-ups tend to pay below-industry salary and compensate for the difference with stock options. If the company fails (which it usually does), your stock options are worth nothing.

- **Limited credibility.** The earliest employees of Google and Facebook have lots of credibility, but let's face it—what are the odds? You may join a start-up, only to have it fail after a few years. And all of a sudden you're back on the job market with some no-name company on your résumé that wasn't good enough to survive. Doesn't sound so appealing, does it?

- **Less mentorship.** Big companies have invested time and money in understanding how to train new employees; start-ups lack both of those things. They probably won't invest in growing you into a great leader in three years because they'll be lucky if they make it that long. Big companies can teach you a structured way of solving problems, under the guidance of more experienced professionals, while those at start-ups are learning on the go. And if your coworkers have never spent time at a big company, they may have never been taught how "real" companies do things.

Notice anything missing in that list? I never listed the lack of perks. The reality is that as much as people are drawn to companies like Google and Microsoft for their flashy benefits, even ex-employees tend not to miss them much once they're gone. Having to scrimp and save due to your meager salary may frustrate you, but a lack of free food tends not to be an issue.

The Ugly

In Ryan's first four years after leaving Amazon for the start-up scene, he'd worked for four different companies. He left one company because of a personality mismatch between him and the CEO. Words were exchanged. It wasn't pretty. The next start-up folded. The third one started to veer in the wrong direction, and he decided to get out before it was too late. Lucky number four is a company he started himself.

Ryan's story is fairly typical of start-up employees. With fewer than 40 percent of tech start-ups making it past four years, rapid job switching is just a fact of life. People joining start-ups should be mentally prepared for this constant change.

The silver lining here is that because your coworkers will have worked at so many places, you'll also be tapped into a broad network of people. It doesn't take long to build the connections to wiggle your way in front of any start-up recruiter.

The Job Title: What Do You Want to Be When You Grow Up?

As a kid, everyone used to ask me, "What do you want to be when you grow up?" Some kids change their answer every few weeks, but not me. I knew I wanted to be a veterinarian because then I could play with puppies all day. I was fairly certain that was, in fact, their entire job. After an unfortunate incident involving my dog and a neighbor's car, I learned that vets also sometimes killed dogs—or, to use their delightful euphemism, "put them to sleep." I decided that, although I would clearly get to play with puppies the rest of the time, it didn't quite make up for the whole dog-murder aspect. So, there I was, yet another 10-year-old with an undecided career path.

At age 14, I decided to enroll in a programming class. ("Decided" is my own personal euphemism for an argument with my mother that went something like "but programming is stupid," followed by her saying "too bad.") Four years later, this was my ticket into Microsoft, and eventually into Apple and Google.

Few, especially outside of engineering roles, have this sort of focus; that's OK. Talk to people, research positions, and start figuring out what's important to you. Ask yourself the following questions to start understanding what career path makes sense.

What Do You Need?

Our society contradicts itself every day. On one hand, we are told over and over again, "money doesn't buy happiness," and we have the disastrous lives of celebrities to drill this into us. On the other hand, we're also told that we really do need that new jacket. Let go of what you think should matter, and be honest with yourself. How much do the following matter to you?

- **Money.** Money may not buy happiness, but it does buy your kid's college tuition. And a house in a nice neighborhood. Or maybe just a nice bottle of wine after a hard week. Does that matter to you? Be careful with looking too heavily at money. While you can be fairly confident that your teaching dream will never bring in the big bucks, you can't be as certain about many other career paths. Passionate, driven people can earn a good living in unexpected ways.
- **Recognition and respect.** Many people who shun the spotlight still desperately crave the admiration of their fellow people. How much do you care about what others think of you? Would you be OK with people giving just a courtesy smile when you say your profession?
- **Work/Life balance.** There is nothing wrong with wanting a nice, stable, 9-to-5 (or in the tech world, 10-to-6) job. You want to be able to enjoy a nice day out on the boat during the summer, and that's fine. Remember, no one went to their grave thinking, "Gee, I wish I had spent more time at the office instead of with my family."

If you find your answers learning away from a job for some reason, ask yourself why. Is there something you need from the job that you wouldn't get?

How Do You Enjoy Working?

I've always thought that, had I lived before computers were invented, I would have majored in architecture. The structure of the work seems similar to what I ended up doing: computer science. I could lead. I would create something. And, while I would have supporting teammates, I'm not glued to someone's side to complete a project. How do you enjoy working?

- **Teamwork vs. independent work.** Everyone loves to say, "Teamwork is the best!," but deep down, you see the problems. Coworkers letting you down or just getting in the way. Needing a consensus just to make a decision. Managing everyone's emotions and expectations. Is this really something you enjoy?
- **Creating vs. maintaining.** While software development is creating a new product, testing is maintaining it. There are no tangible results of your work; it's more like pulling up the plug in a sink while the water's still running. It'll just keep coming and coming. How important is it to feel that you built something? Remember that even "maintenance" jobs (like being a surgeon) can have huge impacts on the world.
- **Leading vs. joining.** Leading is great, but it's the joiners who get their hands dirty. Do you want to lead, with all the joys and responsibilities that come from that? Or would you rather relax a bit more and join someone else to accomplish a task?

What Are You Good At?

Even if you don't know what field you want to go into, you probably have an instinct as to what your skill set is. Which of the following are your strengths?

- **Numbers.** Numbers come more easily to some than to others. Are you the kind of person who can understand real-world word problems and whip up a spreadsheet to demonstrate?

- **Writing and communication.** Don't worry about prose and poetry; it's rarely relevant to the professional world. It's more important to be able to communicate effectively, both in speaking and in writing.
- **Creativity.** Creativity stretches beyond artistic skills; it's also about how you solve problems. When faced with an issue of releasing a software product in China, can you brainstorm other revenue streams to dodge the nearly 100 percent piracy rate?
- **People skills.** Being good with people is more than just being likable (though that's certainly part of it). It's also about reading people, knowing how to encourage them, and knowing when you might be pushing them too hard. Those who are especially good with people may find themselves well suited for management positions.

Most people's college majors have little to do with their eventual career path, so don't feel constrained by your major. Your skill set is so much more than your raw factual knowledge. Analyze your success and failures. Think through actual projects or jobs where you've been particularly happy or unhappy. What was it that made the difference? The answers to these questions will help point you in the right direction.

And You're on Your Way . . .

On my last day at Google, I packed up my final belongings in a single box and was reminded of everything that's great about tech companies.

The Pranks. My teammates had decorated every inch of my desk with pink tissue paper. Even the bottle caps, which we used to pelt each other with, were individually wrapped. Rather than leaving a gap in the tissue paper for my monitor screen, they had taped up a printout of my Facebook page—only they had replaced my smiling face with a Photoshopped picture of me in a princess dress. With wings. They must have spent hours doing this, but no one would have batted an eye. This sort of prank is normal for the cultures of most tech companies.

The Fun. No one batted an eye, either, at having a few cocktails to celebrate my last day. I lined up a drink shaker, a few flavors of Absolut, and mixers that were borrowed from the company fridge. I began taking orders. Just because it was my last day didn't mean that I was not going to contribute some good, honest work.

The Impact. I spent my final day (pre-cocktails, of course) preparing a document about my work to facilitate someone else taking over my responsibilities. I explained the current progress, challenges, and the relationship with our external partners. I knew that I had contributed tangible value to the team, and to the company. One day, our I'd-tell-you-but-I'd-have-to-kill-you product would launch, and I couldn't wait for that day to come.

The Network. People stopped by regularly to wish me well and ask me what I was off to next. The truth is, other than a vacation to Costa Rica, I didn't know. I wanted to set aside some time to travel, something that I didn't get the chance to do after college, and then I would look for opportunities at start-ups. They said to keep in touch, and they meant it. A few suggested that they, too, were considering leaving and wanted me to let them know what I was up to. Hint, hint?

As much I enjoyed my experience at Google, and at Microsoft and Apple, I knew that I'd never return to a big company. They had helped grow me as an engineer and as a businessperson, and had given me the credibility to work almost anywhere, but I knew that I belonged at a smaller company. I bade them all farewell, and went on my way.

Never failing to have the last word, though, my teammates left me with a final remainder of my days with them. They snuck an annoyatron—a tiny device that emits beeps at random for the sole purpose of driving someone crazy—into my car. I drove for months unsure of what the beeps meant and if my car was on the verge of breaking down. Finally, I found the gadget affixed to the underside of my seat, and recognized it immediately. I had started the Battle of the Annoyatrons months earlier, and they had ended with a simple act on my final day. Touché, team, touché.

Chapter 2

Advanced Preparation

I didn't mind answering the same questions for hours on end. And I didn't mind the fact that I never even got a chance to eat lunch because the line to talk to me was so long. What really bugged me about representing Google at career fairs were the chemical engineering majors.

I know, that's unfair. There were others like them: bioengineering, material science, physics, and so on. A quick glance at their résumé would reveal nothing for which they were especially well suited. Sometimes I wanted to ask them, *Is there any reason you're talking to me other than "Oh-my-god it's Google"? Why technology? Why you?*

But I wouldn't. Instead, I'd politely smile and offer a canned response of, "I'm not sure what the best match would be for your background at this time, but we'll keep your résumé on file in case anything comes up." This is kind of like telling someone you meet at a bar, "How about I get your number, and I'll call you instead?" I've used both techniques, and let me tell you, they work great!

It's not that you can't find a role for a chemical engineer, but until Google starts its own chemistry lab (and I'm not holding my breath), a chemical engineering degree alone probably won't be your ticket into the company. The eager chemical engineer—or English literature major—needs to find other avenues to prove that they have what it takes to be a "Noogler."

What Can You Do: An Overview

Recruiters want to know two things when they pick up your résumé: Where would you fit at our company? And would you do a good job? If a recruiter can't identify answers to those two things, then your résumé goes in the trash pile. Your goal, therefore, is to get the experiences and background that will answer those questions:

- **Develop a track record of achievement.** Recruiters want to see that you have a pattern of setting ambitious goals and accomplishing them. Your successes could be in academics, project work, volunteer work, employment, or athletics.
- **Learn to write and speak.** Communication, whether written or oral, is vitally important to your career success. If you aren't comfortable with public speaking, get practice with it. If your writing is weak, take a writing course, or start a blog to get more practice. You don't need to be able to do dramatic readings or write elegant prose, but you do need to be able to write in a way that is clean and professional.
- **Emphasize depth over breadth.** As a college student, I didn't play sports or act or sing. I had two college activities—teaching and representing Microsoft on campus—and I poured everything I had into those. Because I put 200 percent into those responsibilities rather than spreading myself thin, I was able to show tangible accomplishments. (Of course, there's a trade-off. The more breadth you have the more likely you are to have at least some relevant skills in any job.)

- **Become a leader.** You don't need to be the president of a club or the manager of your team (though those are nice, of course), but find *something* you can lead. Kevin, now a Google employee, led the fund-raising process for a local entrepreneurship club. His team of three raised 17 percent more money than the year before!

- **Find a mentor (or become a mentor).** Even if it's not an official mentorship arrangement, find someone who is five or more years ahead of you whom you can contact for advice. That person will offer you insight into their career and, one day, may even help connect you with opportunities.

- **Develop a tangible skill.** You'll position yourself best for these companies if you develop a specific, tangible skill. If you want to be a marketer, learn about marketing. If you want to be in sales, help a local organization raise money. Without a tangible skill, you'll likely blend in with everyone else—everyone else who's waiting at the door to be let in.

- **Learn about technology.** If you think you want to work at a tech company but don't know much about technology, now is a great time to start reading web sites like TechCrunch and CNET, as well as company-specific blogs. Think about what the major topics are—social networking, mobile applications, cloud computing—and ask yourself, who are the leaders in this field, and why? In what ways are these fields changing technology, and therefore the world?

Academics

You know Google—that company famous for wanting Ivy Leaguers with at least a 3.7 GPA? When I joined Google, my team of eight people consisted of three people without a college degree. And our next college hire, well, his GPA wasn't too hot, from what I hear.

Academia is merely *one* way to distinguish yourself, and there are plenty of other ways. So if your GPA, or your school, doesn't stand out, look for additional avenues. Besides, you'll need to excel in multiple areas to get your résumé selected.

Elite Schools: What's in a Name?

A degree from an "elite" college doesn't get you in the door, but it does make it easier for you to get noticed. If you go to a smaller or lesser-known school, there are still plenty of avenues.

Ben, a student at a small liberal arts school in Indiana, got recommended for a Microsoft internship through his professor. Once he was in the door, his college name stopped mattering, and it all came down to his interview—and his internship. "After I finished my internship, they worked hard to recruit me for a full-time position," Ben says. His coworkers couldn't care less about what college name was on his diploma.

If your school isn't nationally known with the prestige of a Harvard or MIT, reach out to your professors or your college's alumni network for connections. Or, you can try to build those connections yourself by seeking out mentors or advice from people in the field.

Picking Your Curriculum: Majors, Minors, and Other Courses

This is where I'm supposed to say, "It doesn't matter what you major in, as long as you find something you love!" But I'm an honest person and I have to tell you: it does matter.

Some majors will simply be easier to get in. The more directly applicable your major is, the better. Computer science, marketing, finance, and accounting majors will have a much easier time getting their résumé noticed than, say, a History major. After all, they have academic experience, and possibly other work experience, that lends itself to a specific role.

But there are all kinds. One day, when I was hanging out at Bill Gates's house (OK, it was for a Microsoft barbeque, but doesn't it sound cooler when I leave that out?), I met an intern who was a music major. Not a dual computer science and music—just a plain old music major. And even he had a directly applicable role: making sound effects for Xbox. He spent his days using ordinary household objects to mimic sounds like a golf ball hitting the grass. I decided that that was, in fact, the coolest job ever.

Learn to Code

While a computer science degree is a fantastic way to get in the door, it's obviously more applicable for programming jobs. And for some reason, not everyone wants to stare at lines of code on a computer screen all day screaming, *"Why isn't this working?!?"* That's cool—I won't judge you.

Even if you're not pursuing software development as a career path, you might find it useful for your tech company career to learn just a bit of coding. It'll help you communicate with developers down the road and offer context to their work. Plus, it'll show a passion for technology that not many candidates can show.

Many universities offer a Programming for Non-CS Majors course, which is a great option for those who aren't as dedicated to the profession.

What About a Minor?

If you choose to major in something less applicable, like history, your minor is your opportunity to add an applicable skill to your résumé. Seek out a relevant minor that complements your path, whether that's finance, marketing, computer science, or one of several other career majors.

A minor is also a great place to prove that you're quantitative. A minor in math or engineering will do that, but so will a minor in economics, finance, or accounting. Whether fair or not, many techies associate the ability to work with numbers as a sign of intelligence (as well as an important job skill), and a minor is your chance to show that.

Get Project Experience

Project-heavy courses are an excellent way to add tangible "accomplishments" to your résumé, even before you have the credentials to get "real" work experience. While other students are trying to dodge these rigorous courses, you should seek them out. You should cherish them for all the grueling, pizza-and-coffee-filled late nights that they bring.

"Remember the projects you work on," Peter Bailey, a software engineer from Denver, adds. "Understand them. Deconstruct them. Save samples of particularly tough problems you've solved. Improve them, even if only on your own machine and on your own time. Because in the future, interviewers will ask you many, many questions about the projects you've worked on. They don't want to know that you're smart. They don't want to know that you can figure out anything with 30 seconds of Google time. They want to know that you can solve problems and produce results—sometime before Christmas. And this holds true whether you're fresh out of college or a 20-year IT veteran."

Grade Point Average: Does It Matter and What Can You Do?

Of all companies, Google is perhaps the most renowned for being GPA snobs. Hysteria surrounds the recruiting process, screaming that Google takes only candidates with *at least* a 3.7. Like most myths, there's some truth to it, but it's mostly just hot air.

The top companies look for the top candidates—people with a track record of success. Your GPA is one point on that graph. But there are other points, too, and you can recover from any low point, whether that's your GPA, your college degree (or lack thereof), or even work experience.

Here is how two candidates with unusually low GPAs scored offers with top companies:

JOHN

John applied to Microsoft with a mere 2.55/4.0 GPA, placing him around the bottom 9th percentile in his class at Dartmouth. Though brilliant, he was never terribly interested in his classes. They were dry and too removed from practicality; he liked to get his hands dirty.

His junior year, he discovered that the robotics team was the perfect fit for his nerdy-yet-practical side. He led the Robotics Club the next year, and came in second in a robotics competition. He showed that he was, in fact, a high achiever, even if homework and tests weren't his thing.

He came off to his interviewers as your classic tuned-out geek, who finally found his passion in building things—or taking them apart. His robotics and other projects gave him plenty to talk about in interviews, and he knew the intricacies of nearly any gadget.

Though he got rejected from more by-the-books consulting companies, Microsoft was thrilled to offer him a position as a program manager.

BETH

Beth started off strong in Berkeley's computer science program, getting As or Bs in every course, until family issues derailed that. Her grades sank, but before that happened, she got a position as a teaching assistant for one of the toughest computer science courses.

Her low-to-mediocre GPA was offset by other successes: president of her sorority, a bachelor's and master's degree in

(continued)

(*continued*)

just four years, serious project work beyond the bounds of her required courses, several TA positions. On top of all that, she got a personal referral to Google, Amazon, and Microsoft from friends who graduated before her.

Between the referrals and her other experiences, Beth had no problem landing a phone screen, and then a full round of on-site interviews. Her interviewers gave her the usual range of software engineering questions, and never gave her GPA a second look. Google, Microsoft, and Amazon were all practically begging for her to join them.

Though their reasons for the low GPA may differ, as well as their compensation strategies, Beth and John found that their GPA really only mattered in the résumé selection process. They were both able to compensate for poor academic performance by excelling in other areas. Companies care about what you can actually *do*, and your interview performance is generally considered a better indication of that than some silly number.

Doctor Who? Getting to Know Professors

My college routine involved weekly coffees with Dr. Max Mintz, a professor whose course was so intense it was featured in the *New York Times*. We'd meet at Buck's County Coffee Co., and he'd order a large iced coffee—none of that crazy Starbucks venti-skinny-half-caf-extra-foam lingo for him. When they ran out of iced coffee (which happened more often than one might expect), newbie baristas would taste a hint of the dry sense of humor that his incoming freshman class so much enjoyed:

"Do you have ice?"

"Yes."

"Do you have coffee?"

"Yes."

"Then you have iced coffee."

"Right away, sir."

Max "went to bat for me" (as he put it) more than once when dealing with certain administrative issues at our university. I haven't had the pleasure of seeing him mid-rant, but he can apparently be quite a formidable force. Since then, he's written multiple letters of recommendations that, while I've never seen any, were strong enough to get me into Google, Microsoft, Amazon, and the Wharton School for my MBA.

Ironically, I didn't do particularly well in his two courses, but I did work my butt off as a teaching assistant for them. The truth is that regardless of how much professors emphasize studying, few professors will be impressed by academics alone.

To get to know professors, you need to go above and beyond:

- **Get involved in their research.** Professors usually welcome assistance with their research projects. For freshmen and sophomores, research positions can also be a great way to get a bit of experience before the biggies like Facebook and Google will open their doors to you.

- **Ask them for help.** If you're doing something on the side—whether it's building a software application or researching a new market—your professors' research may intersect your project. Asking them for guidance is a win-win; you get expert advice, and they get to geek out on a novel application of their favorite topic.

- **Become a teaching assistant.** Not only do you (usually) get paid for this, your professor gets to see you "in action." This makes for a much stronger letter of recommendation if you need one down the road.

- **Lunch, coffee, or office hours.** Many universities offer some sort of "take your professor to lunch" program. If yours doesn't, you can seek your professor's suggestions on course selection or career direction over coffee or during office hours. Like Max, professors are usually much friendlier than they may appear in the classroom.

A strong relationship with your professors can offer you powerful recommendations as you look for jobs, as well as guide you through your academic and professional career. Set a goal to get to know (at least) one professor each semester; it'll pay dividends for years to come.

Work Experience

While we may hope that our bosses are our best advocates, we need to face facts: our bosses have their own agenda. That's casting it in a very negative light, of course. Many bosses will be unselfish and help you move up in the company, or out to a better position. After all, the vast majority of MBAs had bosses who wrote them great letters of recommendation that ultimately led to their departure from the company.

Nonetheless, while you can usually trust your boss with having the best intentions, there are limits to this. You are your own best advocate, and you—not your boss—must map out your career from day one.

Make an Impact

A good employee does everything that's assigned to them; a great employee asks for more. Perhaps the best thing you can do to get a great next job is to do a great job in your current one:

- **Think broadly.** If you're in an engineering role at a web-based company, is there additional debug information you can log? You probably (or hopefully) work with testers; how can you make their lives easier? The more people that

you impact, the better your peer reviews will be and the more
the company will value you.

- **Be really, really good at what you do.** This doesn't mean
  that you have to double your time at work. Perhaps it's merely
  a matter of shutting off other distractions, or perhaps it's a
  matter of being extra careful.
- **Solicit feedback proactively.** Don't wait until your midyear review to solicit feedback. At that point, your manager
  may be so overwhelmed that she writes your feedback hastily,
  at best. Asking for feedback early and frequently will demonstrate maturity, while also ensuring that you are able to
  quickly correct any issues.
- **Learn about other teams.** Understanding the broader
  context of the company's roles will be useful when you want
  a more senior position; for example, if you're a developer,
  learn about what program managers do. If you're in sales,
  learn about marketing. Even a little bit of exposure will help
  you a lot. It'll show you to what other roles are doing and
  how they all fit together.

Become a Generalist

The best program managers, the best marketers, and the best developers have something in common: they each understand the others' roles. The marketers are figuring how to position and price a
product, while the program manager designs user specifications and
passes them down to the developer. It's all interconnected in the
great circle of product development.

Start from your role and work outward: who (outside of
your own position) do you interact with on a regular basis? Make
a point of grabbing lunch with them to understand their role.
How do they make decisions? What do they do on a day-to-
day basis (you know, when they're not with you)? Understanding
the roles around you will enable you to perform better at your

own job by offering greater context, while also offering you transferable skills.

Size Matters: Quantify Your Impact

No matter how happy you are in your current job, with any luck, this role will wind up as a stepping-stone to a new position or to a new company. Suddenly, all your years of work get mashed into a tiny five-bullet box on your résumé and you picture yourself with a T-shirt saying, "I slaved away for five years and all I got were these lousy bullets."

Your five-bullet box should be planned while you're working, not after you leave. Seek out measurable, tangible accomplishments. Build something, create something, lead something. If you've tackled a major issue for your company, can you quantify its impact in terms of dollars, hours, or reduced sales calls? Seek out this information when it happens to ensure that you can get the most precise, accurate data.

Part-Time Jobs and Internships

Some students lift boxes at the university mailroom during the year and bus tables during the summer; others go do something a little more . . . "interesting." I don't think I need to tell you which role will help you more.

My first "techie" job was doing web development and design for the Penn Medical School the summer before I started college. The pay—$12 per hour—wasn't bad for my age but more importantly, I had a position that was actually specialized to my background. Exactly one year later, I was an intern at Microsoft getting paid, let's just say, considerably better.

Of course, not everyone will be so lucky (and I was, indeed, very lucky), but my having an "interesting" job at a relatively early age played a critical role as well. I doubt that my future manager would have looked as fondly upon a waitressing job.

There are lots of interesting jobs you can take—paid, unpaid, and, well, underpaid. Whether you're looking for a part-time position during the school year or for a summer job, you can get an interesting, résumé-building position through the following:

- **Help a professor out with research.** Many freshmen and sophomores can land research assistantships with professors, where you might code (if you're a computer science major) or do other field-specific jobs.
- **Contact a start-up.** There's nothing a young start-up loves more than a bit of free labor. One start-up I talked to had 30 interns—and only 12 employees! Offering to help out a start-up for free can give you fantastic experience. If you really need the money, you can always split time between a start-up and a paid but "boring" job like waiting tables.
- **Volunteer for a nonprofit.** Like start-ups, nonprofits are usually cash strapped and desperate for help. See if you can help them out with something, whether it's coding, fund-raising, or advertising. You'll not only learn marketable skills, but you'll meet other volunteers who may have full-time jobs—jobs at companies who could, one day, hire you.

Remember that experience builds on itself. I never would have gotten to Microsoft if I hadn't been a Photoshop monkey for a summer. And I never would have gotten to Apple if I hadn't been at Microsoft. And I never would have . . . well, you get the point. Your path to getting your dream internship junior year starts freshman year, or even before.

Extracurriculars and the Checkbox People

When I was in high school, my mother used to refer to certain classmates as being "Checkbox People." You know the type. They take all the "right" classes, play all the "right" sports, and join all the "right" clubs. With over 30 percent going to an Ivy League university, my high school was brimming with them. And in a very controlled environment, these students would do exceedingly well.

As much as I loathed the Checkbox People, they were doing something right. They (or my high school) knew how to position themselves for success, even if their alleged passion for theatre was faked.

Things aren't so different now. Not all extracurriculars are created equal. Some show more intelligence, some show more creativity, and some show more leadership. What's right for you depends on your background and, of course, what you enjoy. This section will focus solely on the résumé-building aspects of extra-curriculars; it's up to you to mesh that with your happiness and other preferences.

Volunteering

Much like I won't delve into selecting activities based on enjoyment (which should absolutely be a factor), I won't discuss selecting volunteer activities based on the value-add to the world. If you choose to volunteer, the way in which the nonprofit or volunteer activity contributes to the world is no doubt important. You can make your own determination on this matter.

With that giant disclaimer in mind, allow me to offer this résumé-specific advice: don't serve soup in a soup kitchen. Don't sort clothes for homeless people. And don't pick up roadside trash. While these may be great activities to do for other reasons, no employer will look at your résumé and say, "So, just how many ladles of soup did you say you could do per hour? We've needed a Senior Soup Ladler around here for a while, and I think you're just the right fit!"

These activities will certainly help in some ways. They'll show that you are eager to help and that you can juggle multiple respon-sibilities. They can help fill employment gaps, and they can expand your network. They won't, however, go the extra mile.

To get the most mileage out of your community service hours, focus on activities that will build your skills, let you explore career tracks, or get initial experience in a field:

- **Sales positions.** Consider helping raise money for a homeless shelter through cold calls and other connections.
- **Marketing positions.** Help a local minority entrepreneurship group figure out how to target their advertising and promotion materials.
- **Software engineering/design.** Ever seen a nonprofit's web site? They could probably use your help. Or what about getting involved with an open source project?

Almost any role that you wish to break into at a tech company probably takes place at a nonprofit as well, so you are sure to find something that adds a little extra "oomph!" to your résumé.

Start Something

If volunteering gives recruiters a reason to call, *starting something* makes them get down on one knee and propose (an interview, that is). Of course, it depends on the scale of the project, your commitment to it, and your role, but it's nevertheless one of the best things you can do to boost your odds.

David, a Microsoft program manager, launched a consulting firm whose clients included Fortune 500 companies. He worked nights and weekends for them, which boosted his résumé and refreshed his coding skills. Although program managers often have trouble getting considered for software engineering roles, David landed interviews with both Amazon and Google. Amazon loved his passion and commitment, and offered him a job as a software engineer.

Provided you have the dedication and time to follow through, starting something can be a great way to make your résumé leap.

It shows initiative, creativity, and a commitment to go above and beyond. And, if your background lacks in particular areas, whether that's leadership, coding, or marketing, launching a business or a web site can be a great way to fill that gap.

If you've got some time to spare, consider pursuing the following paths:

- **Launch a business.** Lots of us have ideas floating around in our heads—why not pursue one of them? If you're a coder, this is a great way to learn something beyond the relatively narrow field of your work experience. If you're not, this can be a great way to boost your tech or field background. You can hire developers or other skilled workers to implement your project from web sites like odesk.com and elance.com.
- **Write a blog.** Writing a blog is a great way to show that you have great writing skills, to increase your "net presence" (making it easier for recruiters to find you), and demonstrate your interest in a field such as technology, media, or gaming. Your blog should be updated at least every week or two, so be sure that you have the diligence to post regularly. This can prove much harder than many people expect.
- **Start a club or organization.** You don't want to form clubs just for the sake of forming a club, but if there's a genuine gap in your area, you may want to create an organization to fill it. Doing so can build your leadership experience, expand your network, and show a proven interest in a new field.

But, be warned: if you don't follow through on your project, it can demonstrate flakiness and potentially burn bridges. Make sure that you are excited and committed to your plans.

Your Questions Answered

Well, There Go the College Hires

Dear Gayle,

I'm a senior in college and as such, you can find pictures on my Facebook profile dating all the way back to my junior prom. This means plenty of pictures of illegal underage drinking, keg stands, dressing in drag, toga parties, etc.

My parents, of course, are mortified and insist that I take down these "irresponsible" pictures. Better safe than sorry, they say. And then they tell me all sorts of stories about their friend's son or daughter who didn't get a job because of one picture ("Just one! And you have so many!"). I'm going to get rejected by Microsoft! The world will end! Aaah!

I think this is all crazy talk. Times have changed, right?
~P. L.

Dear P. L.,

Yes and no. But mostly yes.

Your Facebook profile is a pretty darn good reflection of who you are, and employers want to learn about you. Drunken party pictures tell them that you drink. Will that be an issue for your employer? Unless you're applying to the Center to Stop Binge Drinking, your employer should not care whether you drink.

How do I know they won't care? Because if they did, they'd never hire any college students.

In fact (and parents everywhere will hate me for saying this), it could even help you. Look, tech companies have too

(continued)

(continued)

many nerds, and they want people who know how to have a good time. Drinking = sociability, right?

I should qualify my statements a bit. There is a chance that your Facebook profile will hurt you. Namely:

1. **You're doing something offensive.** Overtly racist or sexist statements are an excellent reason for a company to reject you.

2. **You're doing something illegal, dangerous, or outright stupid.** That is, really illegal—not something relatively common like underage drinking. If you're shooting heroin, or beating someone up, that will give them a real, legitimate cause to be concerned.

3. **Your interviewers think like your parents.** Your parents think drunken pictures are unprofessional. There are other people that think like your parents. Therefore, your interviewer might think drunken pictures are unprofessional. Hey, stranger things have happened. But then again, such interviewers probably aren't going around Facebook stalking people, and if they were, they'd realize that what you're doing is completely normal.

That said, if you're really concerned, you can always slap on a reasonably professional profile picture and secure your pictures so only your friends can see them. And while you're at it, block your parents. That'll solve one part of the problem, right?

~Gayle

Will Code for Food

Dear Gayle,

I'm a freshman in computer science and I know I need some real work experience. I could get an internship at a startup, but I also need to earn a bit of money. And that's where the problem comes in. The companies that will hire me don't pay, and the ones that pay won't hire me.

I don't need a ton of money—just enough to pay for basic expenses like dinners and stuff with friends. Am I out of luck? Plan B is to work as a waitress, which I know won't exactly do wonders for my résumé.

~U. B.

Dear U. B.,

I suppose it wouldn't help if I said, "Look harder," would it? OK then. If you can't find a paid internship in your area, why not look outside your area?

Outsourcing does not just mean shipping projects off to India. People outsource stuff *within* the United States, too, and you can get on the favorable side of that.

Sign up on a site like odesk.com, elance.com, or rentacoder.com and bid on some projects. If you win a few smaller contracts and do well on them, you can gain the credibility to get a more sustained summer contract.

You'll get paid, and you'll get résumé-building experience. It's everything you wanted, right? The smaller projects can be listed in your "Projects" section, while your longer projects can be listed under "Employment."

(continued)

(continued)

> Remember that because your goal here is to get experience for your résumé, be sure to explain the situation to your temporary bosses. You may need their permission to list the project on your résumé, and to potentially ask as a reference.
> ~Gayle

The Un-Manager

> Dear Gayle,
> I'm currently working at large software company in Southern California. Things aren't going so well at the company (layoffs, etc.), so it doesn't look like a management position is in reach anytime soon. That's OK, though, sort of. I'll likely be leaving the company in a year, and relocating to northern California, where there are more career opportunities.
> Even if I switch companies, though, will I be able to get a management position without prior experience?
> ~W. H.

> Dear W. H.,
> It depends. What do you call prior experience?
> It's certainly much easier to get a new position when you've already held that title. Otherwise, you need to prove not only your value to the company, but also your ability to accomplish something new.
> However, you may be able to get much of the experience you need, even if you can't win the title. Ask your current manager for more leadership responsibilities. You can even take advantage of the poor situation—explain that you

recognize the company and the team are under some stress, and you'd like to help out by leading a subteam to do X. You won't get the title for that, but you'll get the experience. And ultimately, that's more important.

When it comes to applying for new jobs, you can't lie about your title, but you can tweak things to show what you *really* did. Your cover letter is a great place to emphasize the management-like responsibilities you took on, while the bullets under the job should focus on your leadership-related accomplishments.

~Gayle

Chapter 3

Getting in the
Door

Think companies like Microsoft, Amazon, and Google are getting
tons of great applicants? Think again. "Hiring managers at Amazon
are spending so much time recruiting these days that they barely
have time to actually, well, *manage*," one technical program manager
at Amazon told me. Employees from other top companies echoed
similar concerns:

- "There aren't enough good engineers in the United States.
  Period. We're like vultures fighting over what little there is
  to eat." (Apple employee)
- "We're always hiring great talent. Always." (Google employee)
- "It's not that we don't get enough good candidates. It's that we
  just don't know who they are." (Facebook employee)

It's true. While you're banging down their door to get in, recruiters
are running around trying to find you.

You might be able to just stand still, dutifully submitting your
résumé online. With a bit of luck and an outstanding résumé, they

just might bump into you and ring you up. Most candidates, however, find that they must get a bit more creative.

The Black Hole: Online Job Submission

I won't sugarcoat this for you; we call it a black hole for a reason. Applying online does not exactly have the best track record for yielding interviews.

But it happens. I got my job at Apple by applying online—of course, I had three prior internships at Microsoft. Kari, a financial analyst at Amazon, applied through Amazon's web site and promptly received one of *those* e-mails—"blah, blah, blah . . . we'll keep your résumé on file." And they did, and later offered her a job. Philip got his job at Bloomberg LP through applying on Monster.com.

I can personally attest to the fact that Google *does* look through its online résumé submission, because I've been previously drafted to screen such résumés. We essentially played a recruiter's version of Duck-Duck-Goose: reject, reject, reject, call!

As random as the process is, you can do a bit to shift the odds just a bit more in your favor.

Making the Best of the Black Hole

To increase your chances of getting a call, make sure you follow every instruction. Needle, haystack: you do the math. With so many applicants to wade through, recruiters and hiring managers may look for any excuse to toss your résumé. If they want your transcript, submit your transcript. If they want your top three desired teams, answer their question. Little mistakes can be fatal.

Second, if the job opening is fresh, apply quickly. Waiting three days to think things over just increases the size of the haystack. Companies may even stop looking after a certain point so that they can make decisions on the early birds.

Third, put yourself in the shoes of the hiring manager. If she does a search through the Applicant Tracking System (ATS), what keywords will they use? Make sure to list these on your résumé. For example, if the role encourages an MBA, you'll want to make sure that you have "MBA" written on your résumé rather than just "Master of Business Administration." You may want to list your education as "Master of Business Administration (MBA), 2010" to make sure your résumé gets picked up by both searches.

Fourth, remember that just because you discover the opening through a job web site doesn't mean you have to apply through it. "If the application mentions the recruiter's or hiring manager's name, you might be able to track down his name to send a personalized note," advises Barry Kwok, a former Google recruiter.

Getting a Personal Referral

Sure, Kari, Philip, and I wiggled our way out of the black hole, but all of our other jobs? Referrals. The same goes for almost everyone I know (with the notable exception of those who came through college recruiting).

Personal referrals are, hands down, the best way to get a job. Not only will a company be more likely to consider someone who's been referred, but you'll also be more likely to find a position that matches your skills and interests. It's a win-win.

Tell Your Friends

When I left Google, suddenly people came out of the woodwork. Start-ups, bigger companies, recruiting firms, positions I've never had (or wanted to have)—they all came calling. I ended up taking a position as VP of engineering at a venture capital–funded start-up without a résumé or formal interview.

My situation is far from unique. If you have a highly valued talent and strong credentials to back it up, you may only need to let your contacts know what you're looking for. People *want* to help.

If you use social networking web sites like Facebook or Twitter, a simple message asking if anyone can connect you to your dream company might do the trick. Otherwise, you can be a bit more aggressive: ask your friends who might work at closely connected companies. You can bet, for example, that your Googler friends know a few Microsofties. It can never hurt to ask!

Make Yourself Known

Got your sights set on a dream company, but can't find a path in? Find an employee at the company and make yourself known. Does she have a blog? Comment on it—or better yet, follow up her blog posts with posts of your own. Does she tweet? Tweet back. If she is asking for assistance, help her in any way you can. Immerse yourself in her community.

Even after leaving Google, I've continued to refer candidates to the company who have done just this. After all, if a person has shown himself to be intelligent, generous, and interested, why wouldn't I return the favor?

Don't go overboard, of course. No one likes a stalker!

The Informational Interview

The informational interview is an informal discussion with a company that is conducted before the recruiting process has even begun. Usually, you approach an employee of a prospective company and seek their advice about the role or company. Though it's called an "informational interview," don't mention the word *interview* when you talk to the employee.

Part of the value of the informational interview is that it's low pressure. An employee can meet with you and offer advice, regardless of whether the company is hiring. They get to "vet" you a bit, and you get to evaluate them and their company.

These informational interviews are very common across tech companies, both for external applicants and for internal candidates wishing to transfer teams.

Make sure to come with good, well-researched questions. The person will not be evaluating your skills extensively, but they will evaluate your personality, communication, and interest. Make sure to write a note thanking them for their time.

After this conversation, they may invite you to apply to their company and even offer to refer you. If not, you can follow up after the interview and ask them what the best way is to apply or to get in touch with a recruiter. If they don't respond with an offer to help, then they are probably not comfortable doing so for whatever reason. You will simply need to use alternative avenues to apply for the position.

Reach Out to Recruiters

In college, I decided that if recruiters didn't want to approach me, then I would just have to approach them. Luckily, recruiters don't exactly hide their e-mail addresses. A quick Internet search with a query like <recruiter *@adobe.com> will turn up recruiters from virtually every major company. Which recruiter would you like to talk to? Microsoft? Google? Amazon? You name it, you got it.

Don't e-mail your résumé yet, though—that's just the first step. "Recruiters can tell if they're being spammed," Kwok reminds us. "It's quality, not quantity. A sincere, well-researched letter that's tailored to our company will go much further than a generic one."

You should always try to contact the most relevant recruiter you can. If you can't find someone who recruits for your desired position, state what position you're interested in, and ask them to put you in touch with the appropriate person. If you know the name of the person you need to speak with or the exact position, even better. The less of a burden you are to the recruiter, the more likely he is to help you.

Alumni Network and Beyond

Personal referrals may also be found in alumni networks, or other "official groups." If you're a student or recent graduate, your school's career services office may be able to help you with searching the alumni directory for a connection.

Other groups might include relevant industry groups, many of which can be found on meetup.com. Get out there—you never know whom you might meet!

Career Fairs

Before talking to Microsoft at the career fairs, students in the know would watch the line for a few minutes. Each employee had his or her own system. Some would put a little mark (which was at times as obvious as a smiley face) to indicate his invite/don't invite decision. Others separated résumés into good and bad piles. Either way, an observant person could learn the system. It didn't do them any good, of course, but it sure was nice to know the decision earlier.

Some candidates walk up with their elevator pitch all prepared: here's who I am, here's what I've done, here's what I'm good at, and here's what I'd like to do.

Other candidates walk up, hand a recruiter their résumé, and just wait for the recruiter to ask them questions. When asked what they want to do, they shrug. "Well, what kind of jobs do you have for my major?"

"When a candidate can't tell me what they want to do, or what they even like doing, that's when there's not a good fit," Raquel Garcia, a senior Microsoft recruiter, says. "Basically it's like I'm giving you a ticket to go anywhere in the world, and you can't even tell me what continent you want to go to."

To maximize your chances of getting an interview invitation, follow these suggestions:

- **Do your homework.** Research the companies you're interested in and know which roles you'd be a good fit for. What do they look for in candidates? How can you address those skills in your conversation with a recruiter?
- **Prepare questions.** Part of your job at a career fair is to show your passion for the company and the job. You should

prepare a few open-ended questions to ask the company. This will facilitate conversation, as well as offer both you and the recruiter the chance to discover if there's a good fit.

- **Prepare answers.** A company might ask you basic questions about your background. You should be able to talk intelligently about your biggest accomplishments and challenges.

- **Practice your elevator pitch.** The first 30 seconds with the staff at a career fair is your opportunity to impress. A strong candidate will be able to succinctly communicate their value-add.

- **Tailor your résumé.** There's no rule that says you can bring only one copy of your résumé to a career fair. If you're applying for different types of positions, create tailored résumés for each position.

- **Dress appropriately.** I once had a candidate wear a T-shirt to a career fair with a sexually themed phrase on it. If he can't act appropriately at a first meeting, what will he be like on the job? Your attire at a career fair should be more or less the same as what you would wear to an interview.

- **Follow up.** If possible, get the business card or e-mail address from the person you talk to, and follow up immediately after the career fair. You should reiterate your interest in the company, explain what you'd bring to the company, and attach a copy of your résumé.

After speaking with hundreds of candidates at career fairs, most blend together in a giant mix of résumés. One candidate, however, stands out: Alex, a precocious sophomore, who brought a portfolio of his project work with him. On two additional sheets of paper, he provided screenshots of his four biggest projects, with lengthier explanations that would head off some of our questions: How did he build it? What did he enjoy? What did he learn? What was the hardest part?

Raquel Garcia loves it when younger students like Alex approach her. "Whenever a freshman comes up to talk to me, I always thank them for doing so. They showed guts in talking to me, and I appreciate that. And they get early feedback on how they can start shaping their career so that, in a year or two, they're ready for Microsoft."

Professional Recruiters

Though usually not open to recent graduates, professional recruiting agencies (a.k.a. headhunters) can assist a more experienced hire in connecting and landing jobs with the right firms. They can add value in five key ways:

1. **Connections.** A good recruiter will have relationships with many companies. This will mean not only that the recruiter can convince someone to pick up your résumé, but he may also know about unadvertised job openings. Before hiring a recruiter, you should assess which companies he works with. Where have his recent candidates gotten offers?

2. **Matching you.** A good recruiter will understand your background and interests, as well as the culture and expectations of her client companies. She may do a better job matching you with a good fit than you could do yourself.

3. **Feedback.** A good recruiter will be able to assess where your weaknesses are with respect to each individual job. By knowing this in advance, you can be better prepared to reassure the company of your qualifications. They can also help you prepare by suggesting questions you should or shouldn't ask or telling you what questions to avoid.

4. **Handling issues.** Once you land the offer, your recruiter can help you with anything, from understanding if an offer is fair to actually helping you negotiate your offer. Because

recruiters get a percentage bonus of your salary (from the company, not you), they have a strong incentive to help you get the best offer you can.

5. **Reopening a door.** Sometimes rejections don't mean that you weren't a good fit for the company; you just may not have been a good fit for the position. "A professional recruiter can sometimes reopen a door in these cases," says BJ Bigley from Big Kind Games.

When Things Get Ugly: What to Watch Out For

While professional recruiters can be enormously helpful, they can also be a waste of time or actually detrimental.

Divya discovered this firsthand when her current manager stumbled across her résumé, sent to her by her own headhunter. "I was considering moving to a smaller company, so I signed up with a recruiting agency. I figured this would be a good way to save myself some time, while increasing the number of opportunities. A week later, my manager called me to his office and passed me a print-out of an e-mail. It had a short note from my own recruiter saying, 'Here's a candidate you should check out,' and my résumé was attached. He didn't know that I was looking for a new job, and this was not how I wanted him to find out." Divya was able to smooth things over with her manager, but things were never quite the same once he knew she was on the way out.

Katy Haddix from VonChurch advises candidates to "beware of any recruiter who won't tell you the name of the company. It's a sign that your résumé will be fired off at random." You should always maintain complete control of where your résumé goes.

Additional Avenues

If you go to a small school in Oklahoma, you may not have the connections—or the job fairs—to give you a helping hand. Hope isn't lost, though. You can still get someone to pick up your résumé, but you may have to work a bit smarter, or harder.

Start Elsewhere

"How do you get into Google? Work for Microsoft," Jason, a Microsoft program manager, jokes. As much as this comment may have been said in jest, it has some truth to it. The best way into a company or role may be an indirect path.

In addition to joining one company so that you can eventually transfer to another, you may want to consider joining your dream company in a less-than-dream job. Technical recruiter Barry Kwok points out that a role like an office manager at a start-up can be an easier avenue into the tech world for those who lack specific qualifications. "At a start-up, office managers do everything under the sun," Kwok explains. "As the company grows, you can begin to specialize in an area like HR. Couple that with an additional night course or two in HR, and all of a sudden you're the perfect candidate for a full-time HR position."

Contract Roles

Companies like Microsoft hire hordes of contractors every year to do everything from testing to development to, yes, even program management. If you're having trouble proving that you have what it takes to earn a full-time position, a larger company might be willing to hire you on a contract basis. Because they can terminate you much easier, there's much less risk for the company.

So what's the catch? The catch is that you're treated as a second-class citizen. No employee stock purchase plan. No health club membership. You don't even get invited to the morale events. And at Microsoft and some other companies, you can only work there nine months per year. Even if the lack of perks doesn't hurt you, the unfortunate attitude of your so-called teammates might. You're not a "real" Microsoftie, you see. (Yes, it stinks!)

In fairness to these companies, it's not their fault that they have this attitude. Believe it or not, they're legally obligated to treat you differently. Microsoft lost a lawsuit years ago because they treated their contractors too much like regular employees, and no company wants to repeat that experience. So that's life.

That said, a contract role can be a wonderful way to have flexibility in your life (nine months on, three months of vacation!) or to experience a company sans commitment. Many contractors who perform well in their jobs do make the transition to full-time employee (FTE). To do so, you need to perform well, build connections, discover open positions, and, yes, interview just like anyone else off the street.

Get Creative

While most candidates wouldn't get much crazier than colored paper to print their résumés, some candidates go a bit further. One candidate applied to Google by affixing his résumé to a giant bouncy ball. Another candidate applied to Twitter by printing his résumé on a cake. It won't help them get the offer, but you can bet someone reviewed their résumés.

These nonconventional applications not only show a bit of creativity, but they also show passion. And in some cases, they can show that you "get" (or don't get) the company or its culture.

As a recruiter for the document-sharing application Scribd, Kwok saw two applicants who used Scribd itself to submit their résumés. Both were interviewed, and one became the company's first engineering hire.

Still want that Google recruiter to notice your résumé? What if you imported your résumé to Google Docs and shared it with her (along with a nice cover letter in the share invitation)? It might not work—but it just might! What have you got to lose?

But be warned: these quirky résumé submissions may turn off the wrong company or recruiter. I would not expect a stuffy *Office Space*-esque environment to be amused by such antics.

Official Groups

In an attempt to reach out to new candidates, many of the biggest firms have created groups on Facebook, LinkedIn, and other web sites. Getting involved in the pages—by both stating your interest as well as helping out other candidates—is a great way to show your interest, as well as your communication skills and personality.

Networking

Some people think of networkers like they think of pick-up artists: sleazy, selfish, and full of cheap relationships. And they're right—many networkers are like that. But those are the bad networkers.

Good networkers understand that quality matters much more than quantity, and that they must cultivate deep relationships by forgetting about the fact that they're "just" networking.

Quality, Not Quantity: How to Build a Network that Works

Networking is not a thing you do when you need it. If you need to connect with a new job, you don't just flip a switch and say, "OK, it's time to network!" By the time you need to build a network, it's usually too late—at least to fulfill that one need.

Networking is an all day, all year sort of thing. You build new connections by being open and interested in other people, and you deepen your connections by focusing on the value that you add to other people's lives. Networking is about what you do when you don't need a network.

Be Giving

Cameron, a former Microsoft program manager, wants more than anything to be a successful entrepreneur. He values building a strong network because he knows how important it is, but he's constantly stretched for time and money. When someone asked him for help reaching out to a former teammate of his at Microsoft, he delayed responding for a week and then said that he wasn't sure he had the time to do that. Later, someone else asked him for help with some technology decisions over coffee. He was very busy that day and said he would get back to them; he never did. While there's no anger or hostility toward him, neither feel especially inclined to go out of their way for him. Unfortunately, neither does anyone else.

People quickly learn when working with Cameron that it's all about *his* needs and *his* desires. It's not that he's trying to be selfish; he's just shortsighted and incredibly focused. People like Cameron never build a network that is of any use to them.

Those who focus on giving—without worrying when they'll get repaid—wind up with hordes of people in their gratitude.

Be Open

Cameron has a second problem with networking: he's too focused. Networking, for him, is about what he'll get out of it. He wants to meet other entrepreneurs, so he focused on meeting other entrepreneurs. If you're an accountant, lawyer, or architect, he doesn't want to have anything to do with you.

The problem with this is twofold. First, you might just need a lawyer or accountant one day. Diversity is good. Second, lawyers and accountants tend to know people outside of their profession.

He's wound up with a tiny, shallow network of like-minded people—not exactly a path to success.

Be the Connector

Medhi is everything that Cameron isn't. He's not only a *giver;* he's a connector. Sure, he'll be happy to chat with you about an idea or make some phone calls for you. But he'll also be happy to share his network with you.

Need to reach out to someone at Company X? Want to talk to someone who does Y? Mehdi knows just the guy—or at least knows how to track him down.

Not only do people feel like they owe him, but they want to help him. And how do you help Mehdi? You introduce him to people. And everyone wants to know Medhi, because he knows *everyone*.

People with friends attract friends. That's how the game is played.

Where to Network

Your network is an outgrowth of your friend circle, your professional circle, and also your online identity. To expand your network, you should be actively cultivating those relationships. Get to know people. Talk to them about what they do and what they're interested in. And find ways that you can add value to their lives.

There are countless places you can network—alumni clubs, sports teams, even bars! But here are some of the most productive.

Immerse Yourself in Start-ups

In many cities, the start-up community is one of the most active and engaging and—lucky for you—often centers around technology. And because many of these people are or wish to be entrepreneurs, they want to build a relationship with you.

Immerse yourself in this community. Go to happy hours, meet-ups, and lunches. Listen to tech talks by local start-ups. If you're an engineer, attend hackathons. Simply by showing your face regularly and talking to people about their jobs, you'll start to build an identity in the community—and a network.

And remember, Kwok says, "If you're working so much that you can't network, you better make sure that your work is really good." You'll need it to push your way ahead of all the candidates who *can* network their way into a job.

Social Networking

Though many people lump Twitter, Facebook, and LinkedIn into the same general category of "networking tools," they serve substantially different functions.

Facebook and LinkedIn help you maintain existing relationships. Generally speaking, you don't start conversations with strangers on Facebook—and if you do, you probably don't expect such connections to develop into professional contacts.

Twitter, however, can help you communicate with existing friends, but it's also extremely effective as a tool to expand your network.

Here's how to make the most of these connections.

LinkedIn

LinkedIn can be used to connect with both friends and professional contacts. One venture capitalist encourages his entrepreneurs to "add everyone they meet with—and add them immediately."

To get additional value out of LinkedIn, encourage your connections to write recommendations for you by writing recommendations for them.

Finally, you should search out groups that are relevant to your interests and get involved in the discussions. Recruiters sure do love to hang out in them!

Facebook

Because Facebook is so good at truly "social" networking, many people overlook its professional value. In reality, Facebook's value to professional networking is expressly *because* it's a social service.

Virtually all of my Facebook contacts are people with whom I have some sort of social relationship, ranging from childhood friends to coworkers with whom I was friendly at work, to friends of friends I've seen on occasion. By and large, all of these people like me (or so I hope).

When I need advice or someone to help me, the first and often only place I turn is Facebook. A single status message is usually all it takes. Now *that* is the value of a social network.

Twitter

If you're willing to put in the effort, Twitter can be an extremely effective tool to connect with people or join in on conversations. Most people fail to use Twitter successfully because they can't expend the sustained, daily effort.

If you think you can do this, I would encourage you to set up a Twitter account and start tweeting relevant thoughts and interesting articles. If you don't have an engineering background, tweeting about technology news (and your reaction to it) can be a great way to demonstrate your interest, as well as to learn more.

If you can maintain a steady flow of posts, then it's time to start building up your "following." Follow interesting and relevant people—they may follow you back. Put a link to your Twitter profile on your e-mail signature, on Facebook, and on LinkedIn. And start connecting with the people you most want to meet by responding to their tweets with your own opinions.

Contributing Online

To truly establish your online profile, you'll want to go beyond the basic social networking tools and become an *online contributor:*

- **Create a web site,** with at least basic information about you. Include your résumé, a picture of yourself, and a list of projects.
- **Start a blog** about technology, or whatever you're interested in. Create a web site, and include your résumé and examples of your work.
- **Write guest blog posts.** Many bloggers are happy to let people write a guest post—less work for them! Guest blog posts are still written under your name and will allow you to link back to your own web site.

- **Answer questions.** When you come across questions on forums (especially field-specific ones) that you know the answer to, respond! Recruiters actually look through people's profiles.
- **Get involved with GitHub,** if you're an engineer. Download interesting software and tools, and see if you can improve them or customize them. If you find bugs, report them back to the original developer.

Taking these actions will allow you to demonstrate your skills even before a recruiter talks to you. Many recruiters source candidates based on their online profile. This is a great way to make a recruiter chase *you*.

Your Questions Answered

Applying from Afar

Dear Gayle,

    I currently live in Chicago, but I will be relocating in two months to San Jose when my wife finishes up her residency. The problem I'm facing is that the smaller start-ups I'm applying to won't even consider me since I don't live in the area. They don't like to pay for relocation, interview travel expenses, etc. How do I explain to them that I'm relocating?

~Y. M.

Dear Y. M.,

    I wouldn't necessarily tell them that you're relocating—I would just act like you're already in San Jose. You should never lie, of course, but you can just tell them on a "need-to-know" basis. As long as you're willing to pay for all travel and relocation expenses, this should not present an issue.

Rather than listing your full address on your résumé, list just "San Jose, CA." Employers don't really need your address for anything anyway until they send out offer paperwork. They will likely just assume your lack of street address is a privacy issue and will just shrug their shoulders. Why not just list no location at all? Because they'll then see "Chicago, IL" for your most recent company and assume that you're still there.

When they call you to schedule an interview, that's when you should tell them the truth: that you're actually not moving to San Jose for another two months *at most*, but you'll be making a trip there in two weeks. Will there be a time then that can work? You'll make your life much easier if you can batch your interviewers into the same week.

Because you're applying to start-ups, there's a very good chance that they can't wait two months. They needed you, well, yesterday. You may need to be a bit more flexible with your move, and spend a few lonely weeks away from your wife.

~Gayle

Distant Relations

Dear Gayle,

Over dinner the other night, my mother mentioned that her friend Eliza had a friend Eric who worked at Facebook. I know it's not exactly a close connection, but I've been trying to get an interview there for months. What's the best way to make this introduction?

~V. R.

Dear V. R.,

So let me get this straight—you want an introduction to a friend of a friend of your mother's (who, for all we know, needs to send you off eventually to someone else). This isn't that distant as far as connections go, but it's tricky because you may have little credibility by the time your résumé shows up at Facebook.

My advice hinges on how well you know your mom's friend.

If you know Eliza reasonably well, you can reach out to her directly. Otherwise, your mother should ask Eliza if it's all right if you e-mail her. At that point, your mother can either introduce you two, or you can just grab the e-mail address and e-mail her directly.

Your e-mail should go something like this:

Hi Eliza,

I hope this e-mail finds you well. I've been working at [current company] as a [current position] for a few years now, and I've just started looking for a new position as a [new job title]. I'm extremely interested in Facebook, and I recently learned that you might have a contact there. If there is any way that you could facilitate that connection, I would be extremely grateful. My résumé is attached as well, in case that's useful.

Thank you!

~V.

Short. To the point. A very, very brief mention of relevancy. Résumé attached. And absolutely no reference to your mother.

Why no reference to your mother? Because your e-mail will, very likely, be just forwarded on to Eric and you don't really want "my mommy helped me" attached to it. It's better to have Eric assume that Eliza knows you directly, not via your mother.

In fact, you should choose all your words wisely. Any e-mail that you write—to your mother, to Eliza, to Eric—will often be just forwarded along to the next step in the chain.

Also, remember that you should never make a connection without *mutual consent*. That means, if you're the introducer, have both people agree to the introduction. In this case, you don't have control over how the you-to-Eric introduction works, but you do have some control over the you-to-Eliza introduction. Ask your mother to get Eliza's permission.

~Gayle

Just Following Instructions

Dear Gayle,

I just attended a career fair at my school and had what I thought was a good chat with a recruiter there. But at the end of the conversation, she told me to apply online.

What gives? Did I misinterpret the tone? What should I do now?

I was, however, able to snag her business card from the stack on the table.

~N. C.

Dear N. C.,

It's unlikely that your recruiter was blowing you off. If she told you to apply online, she probably told everyone that.

(continued)

(continued)

What's probably going on internally is that paper résumés are difficult to deal with. People are spread out, and sheets of paper are just not an effective way to manage content. So, HR is now pushing all the recruiting online. It's a bit disconcerting, but—if handled properly—it doesn't have to hurt you at all.

Do as your recruiter said and submit your résumé online, and then follow up with her. Thank her for the wonderful conversation and throw in a few unique details to remind her of your conversation. You are writing, essentially, a cover letter, and you should handle it as such. Tell the recruiter why you're a good fit ("As we discussed earlier today, I've built . . ."). Finally, explain to her that you applied online as she instructed, but you also wanted to attach your résumé here for her reference. If she could give you an update as to your status and/or keep an eye out for your application, that would be fantastic. You are confident that you would be a great match for the company, and you look forward to hearing from her soon.

Make sense?

~Gayle

Chapter 4

Résumés

Just three months into my freshman year of college, I gave Microsoft my résumé—all three pages of it. Large blocks of text recounted in excruciating detail the features of the three C++ games I'd created. Under "Work Experience," I reported every web page I had designed as though each shed some unique and fascinating light on my credentials. The recruiter tossed my résumé aside without a second glance.

With a bit of persistence but mostly dumb luck, I did in fact wind up at Microsoft that summer. My résumé drifted its way to the desk of perhaps the one person who would give me a chance, and he just so happened to need an intern. Jon had a penchant for the less traditional. My three-page faux pas didn't faze him.

I am fairly sure that I exhausted all luck right then and there. Résumés are an art form, and what I submitted was the equivalent of a four-year-old's crayon drawing: cute, perhaps, in an incredibly clueless way.

A good résumé clearly highlights a candidate's relevant skills. It must present the candidate in the best possible light because, after all, it is one's first chance to persuade the reader that she is the best candidate for the job.

Six Hallmarks of a Powerful Résumé

A powerful résumé should leap off the page saying, "Me! I'm the one you want to hire!" Each and every line should contribute to the employer's wanting to hire you. Why, then, does a candidate list his vague and totally unprovable love for running? One has precious few lines on a résumé, so unless you're applying to work in a health club, skip the fluff.

Before submitting your résumé, go through each line on it and ask yourself why it would help convince an employer to interview you. If you can't give a reason, there's a good chance it shouldn't be there.

The six hallmarks of a powerful résumé is a checklist that your résumé should pass with flying colors. Does yours?

1. Accomplishment Oriented

If your résumé reads too much like a job description, then there's a good chance you're doing it wrong. Résumés should highlight what you did, not what you were *supposed* to do.

Example:

- Responsibility oriented: "Analyzed new markets and explored potential entrance strategies for China division."
- Accomplishment oriented: "Led entrance strategy for Foobar product in China, and successfully persuaded CEO to refocus division on the enterprise market, resulting in a 7 percent increase in profits"

The accomplishment-oriented résumé packs a much stronger punch. Everyone wants an employee who "gets things done."

Watch out for words like *contributed to, participated in,* or *helped out with.* These are good signs that you have focused more on responsibilities than accomplishments. After all, someone at Microsoft could say that they "contributed to the implementation of Microsoft Office." But what does that really say?

2. Quantifiable Results

Ever seen an advertising campaign that says, "A portion of our profits is donated to charity"? The convenient thing about that statement is that it could be 0.0001% and it's still technically true.

This is what I think about every time I see a résumé that says "reduced server latency" or "increased customer satisfaction." If you really did this (and it had a remotely meaningful impact), why can't you tell me how much?

Quantifying your results makes them meaningful by showing employers the impact that you had. If you've implemented a change that reduced company costs or increased profits, employers want to hire you.

For business roles, quantifying results with dollars will make the strongest impact. However, if this isn't possible, you can instead quantify the results with change in employee turnover, reduction in customer support calls, or whatever metric is the most relevant. You may want to consider offering the percentage change in addition to (or sometimes instead of) the absolute change.

For technical positions, it may be more impactful to quantify some results in more technical terms: seconds of latency, number of bugs, or even an algorithmic improvement in big-O time. However, be careful to strike a balance here: while your accomplishments may be impressive to a fellow engineer, a less technical HR individual might be the one reviewing your résumé. You want to make sure that your résumé impresses everyone.

Example:

- Original: "Implemented crash reporter and used results to fix three biggest causes of crashes."

- Newly quantified: "Implemented crash reporter and used results to fix three biggest causes of crashes, leading to a 45 percent reduction in customer support calls."

Before, I understood that you did something reasonably important but I didn't understand how important. The quantified revision, though, leaves me with a "wow!"

3. Well Targeted

Back in the days of typewriters, a generalized résumé could be forgiven. Editing a résumé was a laborious process, and candidates frequently made 200 photocopies and sent off the same résumé to every company. A well-targeted résumé undoubtedly performed better, but it wasn't as strictly required.

Now, with résumés being easy to tweak and rarely even printed, tailoring your résumé to the position is a must. Competition has heated up, and this extra bit of work is necessary to put your résumé on the same playing field, let alone jump out.

Your résumé must be tailored to the position, and potentially the company as well. This is especially important for job switchers. For example, if you're applying for a technical lead position after years of being a software engineer, you'll want to mention the time that you led the design of a new feature. Or, if you're applying to a start-up that you know is facing customer support issues, you'll want to emphasize your prior experience in handling upset clients.

Luckily, figuring out how to target your résumé isn't especially hard. Discovering information about the company or position is usually quite straightforward; you merely need to check their web site and/or the job description. Ask yourself, what are the company's biggest issues? How would my role impact those? Even if you haven't solved the exact problems the company faces, you hopefully have skills one would need to solve them.

4. Universally Meaningful

Some résumés are so littered in technical jargon that it's hard to discern meaning from them. Technical jargon need not mean anything computer related; it could be fancy sales terms, marketing terminology, or even internal expressions. Candidates at big companies are often the worst at this! They spent so long in their own companies that they forget that terms like S+ aren't actually widely known (yes, Microsofties, I'm looking at you).

Your résumé should be meaningful to recruiters as well as to your future managers and teammates. Avoid acronyms, and translate highly technical terminology to plain English. Explaining the impact or goals, particularly in a quantifiable way, can help laypeople understand your value. You still can't please everyone, and that's OK; just make sure that everyone will get the "gist" of your résumé.

That said, some terms are more understandable than one might think. Google recruiters in Seattle certainly knew what it meant for a Microsoft employee to have been promoted from a Level 60 to a Level 63 during her career.

5. Clean, Professional, Concise

Many recruiters will toss your résumé away for a single typo. They figure that they have so many résumés to go through; why waste time on someone with poor communication skills?

Tech companies tend to be a bit more forgiving, due to their less formal atmosphere and as well as their large international workforce. However, that's no excuse for sloppiness, particularly in communication-heavy roles.

Make sure to check your résumé thoroughly for the following potential issues:

- **Conciseness.** Avoid large blocks of text on your résumé; people hate reading, and will generally skip right over paragraphs. Your résumé should be a collection of bullets of around one to two lines.

- **Spelling.** With all due credit to Mrs. O'Connor, my fifth-grade teacher, here's a useful tip to check spelling. Our minds have a tendency to read through spelling mistakes if we know what word to expect. Try checking for spelling mistakes by reading your résumé *backwards*.

- **Grammar.** You can use Microsoft Word's grammar checker, but don't rely exclusively on this. If you are not a native English speaker, make sure to have a native English speaker—one who is strong in grammar and spelling—review your résumé.

- **Margins.** You're not fooling anyone with the 0.5-inch margins. Your margins should ideally be one inch, but certainly no less than 0.75 inch.

- **Normal fonts.** Use a standard font, like Times New Roman or Arial, and don't use fonts smaller than 10 pt. Comic Sans is never acceptable.

- **Consistency.** You can use either commas or semicolons to separate items in a list, but be consistent. End either every bullet with a period, or none. Make sure that your formatting is consistent in terms of bold, underline, italics, and the like. Your formatting decisions are often not as important as being consistent with them.

- **White space.** Using ample white space will make your résumé easy to read. Recruiters have to deal with enough in their day; don't add to strain with a crowded résumé.

- **No first person.** Although it can be tough, avoid using *I, me,* or *myself.* Use the third person throughout your résumé, with the exception of the objective statement, where first person is more expected.

6. Well Structured and Clear

When a recruiter picks up your résumé, her eye jumps to certain things. She wants to know your education (school, degree, major, and graduation year) and your professional experience (companies, titles, length of employment). For software engineering jobs, she may also look for a set of technical skills.

Remember that the path of least resistance for the recruiter is always to toss the résumé. If she can't find the information she's looking for, there's a good chance she'll just toss your résumé so she can move on to the next candidate.

Beyond simply structuring your résumé in an intuitive way, you can make small formatting changes to make the best stuff jump out. Consider the following (very abbreviated) résumés for the same candidate:

Bob Jones (Résumé 1)	Bob Jones (Résumé 2)
Software Design Engineer (2008–Present) Microsoft Corporation ■ Designed modules for Visual Studio.	**Microsoft Corporation** (2008–Present) Software Design Engineer ■ Designed modules for Visual Studio.
Software Engineer (2006–2008) Intel (Santa Clara, CA) ■ Improved embedded code on chips.	**Intel** (2006–2008) Software Engineer ■ Improved embedded code on chips.
Software Developer (2000–2006) Cisco ■ Shipped 8 products over the course of 6 years.	**Cisco** (2000–2006) Software Developer ■ Shipped 8 products over the course of 6 years.

While these résumés convey the exact same information, résumé 1 emphasizes that Bob held software engineering roles. That's very relevant, of course, but it's hardly a highlight of the résumé. Résumé 2, however, emphasizes the fantastic company names: Microsoft, Intel, and Cisco. Which one do you think will pack a strong punch?

When you are writing your résumé, ask yourself: what will differentiate me the most from other applicants? What will make the recruiter put my résumé in the "yes" pile? Ideally, this information will be so obvious that even with a mere glance, someone cannot miss it.

The Structure

Although we usually see résumés structured chronologically, there is an alternative structure: the functional structure. Under the functional structure, your résumé is grouped into categories such as "Leadership," "Engineering," and "Sales." Each category lists your relevant accomplishments, often without dates or positions clearly labeled. Many résumé writers have recommended functional résumés for those whose job titles don't match their true accomplishments, or for those with significant job gaps. Functional résumés tend to mask those issues.

However, recruiters tend to be wise to this strategy and will spend their time trying to figure out what you want to hide—or, more likely, just toss your résumé since it's not worth the trouble. Functional résumés may be powerful in theory, but with so many people having such a strong distaste for this structure, it's probably not worth the risk. If you must separate your accomplishments by skill set, I would recommend a cover letter instead.

We'll focus on standard résumé format: the (reverse) chronological structure. Chronological résumés tend to almost always have at least an Employment (or Work Experience) section and an Education section, but may also include an Objective, Summary, Technical Skills, or Projects section. Which sections you choose to include depends on your skills, background, and desired position.

The Objective

I've probably gotten only one résumé with an objective that was interesting—and in this case, interesting isn't necessarily good: "to dive at such depths into my subjects and work that I am no longer a prisoner to the confines of my mind and I am instead engaged in the rapture of understanding." I'll save you some time and tell you what she was trying to say: she wants to learn stuff. No one was impressed.

While this objective might be unusually philosophical, most objectives do little other than waste precious space. Objectives are not necessary and should be used only if it adds important information.

For example, if you were previously in product management but would like to focus your job search on marketing roles, an objective could be valuable to point recruiters in the right direction. If, however, you're applying for a sales role and your prior position was also in sales, you probably don't need to specify this. Most software engineers do not need objectives, as their experience is clearly indicative of such a role.

An effective objective statement will not only direct your résumé toward the right roles, but will also tell the reader why he should hire you:

> Project management and marketing professional with 10 years of experience growing new business unit from $10 million to $100 million seeking a position as a marketing lead in consumer software.

If you don't need to redirect your résumé to a new role, you should probably stick to just a summary or a list of key accomplishments.

Be aware that objectives may prevent you from getting roles that could have interested you. What if that program manager lead position would have been perfect for you, but the recruiter doesn't contact you because you said you were interested in marketing roles?

Summary (or Key Accomplishments)

While summaries can wow the reader, they're usually so vague that they have no impact at all. Roy, an ex-Microsoft and current Google developer, says, "I would never look at a résumé and say, 'Well, this person says he's a go-getter. Let's hire him.' It's like putting 'Loves to Laugh' on a Match.com dating profile. No one's buying it."

Your summary should read much more like key accomplishments—so much so, in fact, that these sections are often called "Summary and Key Accomplishments."

The following objectives will demonstrate your value-add to the prospective company:

- "Software engineer lead with several years' experience implementing large back-end systems in Java and C++, including three as a lead/team manager; led re-architecture of critical system that serves 50 million requests per month, reducing request latency by 20 percent; designed new API for financial product used by 5 of the 10 biggest banks, which accounted for an additional $10 million in revenue; awarded the prestigious 'Green Sticker' award, given to the top 5 percent of engineers based on total impact to firm."

- "Program manager with five years of experience leading feature design of enterprise-oriented products; proposed solution and built team to solve number one cause of customer complaints, and completed project three months ahead of schedule; reduced development costs by 35 percent by creating plan to merge related products into one, more generalized product; oversaw integration of acquired technology by leading 17 developers and 9 testers from two companies, resulting in an additional $50 million of sales."

Work Experience

For most candidates, the Work Experience section is the most important section of their résumé. Your work experience should, at the minimum, list your job title, company name, firm location, and dates of employment. If you are working for a large firm with many products, such as Microsoft or Amazon, you may also want to list your team.

Your most recent job should have around four or five bullets of one to two lines each. Each bullet should focus on your *accomplishments*, not your responsibilities, and should be backed up with numbers whenever possible.

If you have trouble creating this section, start with listing your biggest accomplishments on a sheet of paper. Remember, though, that what was the most impressive to you or your team, who understand the full complexities of the problem, may not be as impressive when described out of context and in a mere 25 words.

How Far Back Should It Go?

Without showing any gaps, you should list only as far as the positions are relevant—and usually no more than three to five jobs. This means that if your career started as an information technology (IT) technician, but you then moved to testing, and then later had a few programming positions, you can probably cut the IT technician. A résumé does not need to be a complete employment history.

Projects

Software engineers with substantial nonwork experience should include a Projects section. For recent graduates or current students, this is a great way to diversify your résumé and show some additional accomplishments.

> **Desktop Calendar** (Fall 2010, Individual Project): Implemented web-based calendar supporting online storage and syncing, meeting invites, and conflict resolution. Python, Javascript, AJAX. 20,000 lines of code. *Awarded "Honorable Mention" in Senior Design Projects.*

If you are not applying for a software engineering position but have other substantial work, you can rename this section with a more appropriate title. For example, if you founded a club that accomplished some concrete goals and led your school's shift to electronic course review, you might make this a "Leadership Experience" section.

Education

Even if you have a 4.0 from MIT, your experience usually matters more than education. Education is a checkbox, but an important one nonetheless.

In addition to the standard items (university name, dates attended, location), your education section should list the following:

- **Major, minor, and degree.** If your major has a nonstandard name, you should explain the curriculum on your résumé—and you can do so in a way that shapes the reader's perception. For example, the University of Pennsylvania offers a major called "digital media design (DMD)," which is a fusion of computer science, communication, and fine arts (think: future Pixar engineers). A DMD student who is applying for a software engineering role at Amazon might describe it as "a computer science–based major with additional courses in design and communications."

- **GPA.** Generally, recent graduates should list their GPA on their résumé if it's at least a 3.0 out of 4.0. If your school lists GPA in a nonstandard way (such as on a 10.0 scale), you should consider translating your GPA to a more understood system, such as class rank.

- **Activities.** Recent graduates should list their most serious (that is, most impressive/relevant) activities on their résumé. Don't list everything you did, though—everyone can have a lot of half-hearted activities, so an extensive list won't impress anyone. More experienced candidates usually will not include activities.

- **Related coursework.** Current students and some recent graduates may want to list relevant courses. Make sure the courses are truly relevant, though. If the course names aren't clearly understandable to someone not familiar with your university, you may want to give them more "user-friendly" names. This is also an excellent section to tailor to each position or company.

- **Awards.** If you received any awards in college, they often will be listed here. You could, instead, include an "Awards" section, but many candidates find that this takes up precious space. Students with low GPAs may find that awards help them compensate for an otherwise less impressive college experience.

While you must always include education on your résumé, this section should get shorter with more work experience. Many candidates with even two or three years of experience list just their major and degree.

What about High School?

High school almost never belongs on a résumé. There are probably only three exceptions to this—and two of them occur only very rarely:

- **Freshmen and sophomores.** Freshmen and sophomores might consider listing their high school on their résumé, but only if they really have nothing better to list. It's unlikely to impress anyone.
- **Building a connection.** In rare cases, you might know that you're sending your résumé to a fellow alum or someone else strongly connected to your high school. One candidate, Mark, included his small private high school on his résumé and wound up interviewing with someone whose daughter attended the same high school. He says it helped them build a connection.
- **A very impressive accomplishment.** If you have some very impressive accomplishments from high school and the only way to include them is to list your high school, this might be acceptable. However, it's more likely that these accomplishments should go elsewhere, such as under an Awards section.

Which Comes First?

The rule of thumb is that education should be listed before work experience for current students (or graduates with no post-college work experience). For everyone else, work experience is listed first.

However, as tech companies are increasingly OK with small deviations, there is some flexibility with this decision. If your education is much stronger or more relevant than your work experience, or vice versa, you could deviate from custom. It is unusual, but the benefits might outweigh the costs.

One candidate whose résumé I reviewed had an electrical engineering degree and had been employed for several years as a software tester. While working full time, he had enrolled as a part-time student at Stanford, where he had recently completed four computer science courses. In this case, I recommended to him that he list his education first. His work experience would usually eliminate him from software engineer; his only saving grace was that he was taking computer science courses at Stanford. What other choice did we have?

Skills

This is a must for technical positions, and often unnecessary for non-technical positions. This section should list any software, programming languages, foreign languages, or other specific skills you know. To avoid a lengthy, disorganized list, it is useful to divide up this list into appropriate categories.

However, just as a native English speaker would never list "English" as a skill, you should not list "obvious" skills such as Microsoft Office. It's assumed. Likewise, familiarity with Windows and Mac can be left out unless you are also listing something less obvious, such as Linux.

Anything on your résumé is fair game, including all of your programming or foreign languages. Animas, a start-up medtech company outside Philadelphia, once interviewed a candidate who claimed to be fluent in Romanian, Portuguese, Greek, and Italian. He mostly did very well, and would have surely received an offer—except that the small company just so happened to have Romanian, Portuguese, Greek, and Italian employees, and they just so happened to be available for an interview that day. Animas didn't care about the languages, but they did care about the honesty.

Awards and Honors

If you have awards or honors, you can choose to list those either with your work experience/education or in their own Awards section. The best decision largely depends on how much space you have and how much you want to emphasize your awards. Are your awards a key differentiating factor between you and other candidates?

Either way, you should list the dates and why you received the award. When your recruiter sees an award like the "Vincent R. Jacobs Award," she has no idea what that means. Your awards should instead be listed as something like, "Recipient of Vincent R. Jacobs Award, given annually to the top woman by GPA out of the 3,000-person senior class." If you can quantify your award to suggest the selectivity, that's even better.

What Not to Include

For positions in the United States or Canada, a résumé should never include race, religion, sexual preference, marital status, or anything else associated with discrimination. Pictures, which are indicative of some these items should also not be included. Recruiters hate these pieces of information, because they expose the company to increased liability.

How Long Is Too Long?

When you go grocery shopping, you read every label, right? No snap decisions for you. You review all the pros and cons, evaluate the ingredients, and read all the great marketing material before you make a decision to purchase. And you do this for all 50,000 products, right? Because that's the informed, savvy consumer you are.

OK, maybe not. If you're anything like me, you probably make some snap decisions based on your initial impressions, only doing a "deep dive" once a product has passed the initial screening process—if at all.

Recruiters are much the same way. They can't afford to read each and every line on a résumé to dig around for the most relevant times. The review process is more like a quick "skim" than actually reading.

So how long should your résumé be? In the United States, your résumé should be as reasonably possible. While senior candidates might be able to justify a two-page résumé, candidates with less than 5 or 10 years of experience should stick to just one page. If you're finding it very difficult to squeeze your experience into those limits, that's not surprising; everyone says that!

In the United States, shorter is generally better. When your recruiter spends only 15 to 30 seconds on your résumé, you want him to think you're an A+ candidate. A one-page résumé forces you to be selective and include just the best stuff. When your résumé gets longer, more and more B or C content gets mixed in. Pretty soon, your recruiter sees you as a B candidate.

In the United Kingdom and other countries, candidates often submit curricula vitae, which can be several pages. Expectations vary by country. Countries with longer résumés as standard may be accustomed to spending more time reviewing each résumé.

How Do I Shorten My Résumé?

Everyone has trouble shortening their résumé. You get attached to your accomplishments, and you just hate to see them wiped off. Try giving your résumé to a friend and ask him or her to cut items, line by line. What do you not need?

Or ask yourself these questions:

- **Do you have more than three prior jobs listed, or 15 years of experience?** If you are an experienced candidate, your résumé need not stretch back much more than 10 or 15 years. Stick to only what's relevant.
- **Do you need to talk so much about your older jobs?** If you have an older job that you'd like to include because, say, the firm has a strong name brand, you only need to spend one bullet on the job. The space allocated per position does not need to match the number of years spent.
- **Can you cut some of your college experience?** Things like coursework and activities can often take up more space than they are worth. Remove these, unless they truly add a new perspective or accomplishment.
- **What does your objective/summary add?** Objectives and summaries often take up three or four lines of text and add very little. Most people could remove their objective and summary and lose very little.
- **Is everything relevant?** Discussing your love for traveling is very rarely relevant, nor is the fact that you think you have strong communication skills. Kill the fluff.
- **Can I be more concise?** Résumés should use bullets with, yes, incomplete sentences. If you have meaty paragraphs and blocks of text, these should be trimmed. You don't need to provide all the details.
- **Is this the best résumé format?** Often, a different format can create much more space. Try experimenting with the format, but don't shrink the font size down too much or remove all the white space. It's there for a reason.

Your Questions Answered

It's a Family Matter

Dear Gayle,

The only school activity I've done is the waterskiing team—and that was just my freshman year of college. I was hoping to get more involved with college activities, but then my father got sick.

I didn't have to take time off school, but I did have to help him out a bit at work. He runs a local chain of jewelry stores, so I've had to do everything from hiring and training salespeople for a new store to reorganizing our accounting system. Being family and all, I didn't get paid a dime (!).

I'm a junior now and about to apply for internships. Is there a way to tactfully explain my family situation on my résumé? It looks rather sparse as is, and it doesn't look like this situation is going to change anytime soon.

~K. C.

Dear K. C.,

While you can absolutely briefly explain your situation if an interviewer inquires, personal details like this do not belong on a résumé. Your résumé is about what you actually did, not your excuses (even if reasonable) for not doing more.

However, you can—and should—list your experience with your father's business on your résumé. No one has to know that it's your father's business and, frankly, it doesn't matter anyway. The good thing, as you said, is that you've done a wide variety of things.

Think through your past couple of years on the "job" and make a list of your most tangible accomplishments. These will become your résumé bullets. Tailor your selections to the positions you're applying for. That is, if you're applying for program manager jobs, your work building a new team for a new store is very relevant, as well as anything else that shows leadership. Then, come up with an appropriate job title. You can be called anything you want (within reason), as long as you clear it with your boss/father.

In the future, ask your father if you can focus your activities on particular aspects of the business that are most relevant to your career. This could be a win-win for you and your father—and even for your future employer.

~Gayle

On the Up and Up

Dear Gayle,

I had a low GPA freshman year—very low. It was 1.93. I've worked really hard and pulled mostly A's, but still my GPA is only a 2.98. That places it just below that 3.0 cutoff that many companies have.

Should I just not list my GPA?

~M. G.

Dear M. G.,

Conventional wisdom is that you don't list your GPA when it's below a 3.0, but I do feel that yours is somewhat of a special case. Your grades now are, in fact, quite good. I worry that by leaving off your GPA, the assumption will be that it's lower than a 3.0.

My advice is that if you have academic awards, like the Dean's List, list those without your GPA. That will remove the employers' assumption when they didn't see a GPA.

If you don't have such awards, you should list your GPA— but only your GPA after freshman year. Something like this will do the trick:

- **GPA:** 3.6 (Junior Year), 3.4 (Sophomore Year)

It'll be plainly obvious what you're doing, but that's not really an issue. The important thing is that your grades are good *now*, and they have been for a while.

When your interviewer asks what happened freshman year, don't beat around the bush. Tell him the truth. You were a bit overwhelmed, both academically and socially, with college. You realized at the end of the year that you really needed to straighten up and focus, and you've done just that.

Personally, if I heard an answer like that, I'd be pretty impressed. You've shown honesty in your answer and maturity in your reaction. Way to go.

~Gayle

But Seriously

Dear Gayle,

I have about two years' work experience in two different roles. I also have three internships from college, plus a double major and a few extracurriculars. I'm having trouble fitting it on two pages, let alone one.

If I need it, I can use more than one page, right?

~R. S.

Dear R.S.,

No.

Well, ok, *if* you need it, sure. But that's one heck of a qualifier—and one that I don't buy into.

Not all recruiters are strict on the "one page" rule, but some are. Do you really want your recruiter's first thought to be frustration?

Even if a recruiter gives a vague "oh, any length is fine" statement, it doesn't mean longer is better. Focus on the best, most relevant accomplishments. You can fit them all one page, I assure you. Diluting them with weaker items will only make you look worse.

~Gayle

Chapter 5

Deconstructing the Résumé

In the previous chapter, we told you what makes a good résumé, and it was things like conciseness, structure, accomplishments, and so on. But seeing a bunch of A+ résumés does you only so much good.

In this chapter, I'll show you two mediocre résumés and one great one. We'll walk through what's good and bad about all three. You will develop a more trained eye to evaluate a résumé and will be better able to apply this thought process to your own résumé.

Though names and some identifying details have been changed, these are all real résumés from real candidates.

Please note: Due to limitations of page size, we will not review the length of the résumé or the formatting. Additionally, for brevity reasons, we have included only excerpts of résumé sections.

Résumé A: Bill Jobs

Objective Seeking a full-time position as a software engineer where I can contribute to the success of the company.	1. *This objective doesn't add anything. All it specifies is that the candidate is looking for a software engineering position, which should be obvious.*
Education **University of Maryland**: Aug. 2008 – Dec. 2010 Master of Science, Computer Science (GPA: 3.93/4.0) **India Institute of Technology**: Aug. 2002 – Jun. 2006 Bachelor of Engineering, Computer Science (GPA: 3.7/4.0)	
?Technical Skills *Technologies*: Java, C, Visual Basic, SQL, REXX, COBOL, Shell Script *IDE/Editors*: Netbeans, Eclipse, VIM *WEB Technology*: Servlet, JSP, PHP, JavaScript, JQuery, Ajax, HTML, XML, CSS, Action Script, Firebug, Hibernate *APIs*: Google Visualization, FusionCharts, PHP, Report Maker *Database*: MySQL, Oracle *Server*: Apache, Tomcat *Source Control*: SVN/CVS *Platform*: Linux, Windows Vista/XP, OS390	2. *The candidate has seemingly listed every technology he's worked with. Most companies don't care at this level, especially the "top" companies.* 3. *This extensive list also raises the question of how comfortable he is with them. Will he be able to tackle questions of these topics?*
Employment **University of Maryland**. College Park, MD (Jan. 2010 – Sept. 2010) Graduate Assistant ■ Implemented back end using Java Servlets. ■ Implemented Servlets to manipulate weather buoy data and generate XML for Fusion Chart to visualize data.	4. *These descriptions are very vague—I can't get a good handle on what exactly he did. What was the goal? What did he accomplish?*

(continued)

(Résumé A continued)

■ Wrote Java scripts to provide rich and dynamic user interface. ■ Assisted in setting up Tomcat server on Linux.	5. *Additionally, setting up a piece of software is hardly an accomplishment compared to other graduate work.*
Around Circa, Inc. Sunnyvale, CA. (July 2009 – Jan. 2010) Web Developer, Intern ■ Designed and implemented SMS service, which allows user to access available online services such as search, connect, and registration through mobile. ■ Implemented the back-end logic using Java Servlet. ■ Designed and implemented real-time analytics using JSP Report Maker and Fusion Chart that generates reports and provides visualization of real-time data. ■ Implemented Hibernate mapping and Java classes to provide clean interface for interacting with database. ■ Utilized JQuery and AJAX to provide dynamic and interactive user interface. ■ Designed and created MySQL database and also wrote PHP script to populate the database with test data. ■ Built Restful API, which allows our IPHONE application to interact with the backend. ■ Developed blog poster using PHP for posting blog on company web site.	6. *He's listed a lot of items here under his job. When you list this many, it almost certainly means that you have a lot of junk mixed in.* 7. *Again, the descriptions are vague. Language like "Implement the back-end logic, which generates a diagram based on a sequence of rules" could be a bit clearer.* 8. *On the bright side, Bill does know to focus on his accomplishments rather than his responsibilities, which is good.*
Projects **Remote Method Invocation System** (Language/Platform: Java/Linux)	9. *Bill's project descriptions are excellent. They provide just the right amount of detail to be useful, without overwhelming the reader.*

Based on classical stub–skeleton design for communication between client and servers, this system takes description of remote object interfaces in form of Interface Definition Language (IDL) and generates stub and skeleton which provides communication support to invoke remote object.	*10. The one thing that would make this slightly stronger is for Bill to list the dates of the projects.*
Distributed Hash Table (Language/Platform: Java/Linux) Successfully implemented Distributed Hash Table based on chord lookup protocol, Chord protocol is one solution for connecting the peers of a P2P network. Chord consistently maps a key onto a node.	
Information Retrieval System (Language/Platform: Java/Linux) Developed an indexer to index corpus of file and a Query Processor to process the Boolean query. The Query Processor outputs the file name, title, line number, and word position. Implemented using Java API such as serialization and collections (Sortedset, Hashmaps).	
Achievements ■ Won Star Associate Award at Capgemini for outstanding performance. ■ Received client appreciation for increasing productivity by developing Batch Stat Automation tool.	*11. He's listed an award, but he hasn't explained the significance. What is Capgemini? What's the award for, and how competitive is it?* *12. Bill mentions that he increased productivity, but by how much? Quantifying his accomplishment would help.*

Assessment

This is very much a mediocre résumé. It's well structured and easy to read, but I have trouble understanding a lot of his work experience. More elaboration and context behind his accomplishments would make them more real.

Résumé B: Steve Gates

Objective To work in a mutually beneficial environment where I can utilize my experience and hardworking nature to overcome obstacles and ensure on time quality deliverable at the same time learn in a highly competitive environment.	1. *Again, this is a fluff objective. Most objectives are. Don't list an objective unless you need to.*
Skills Project Management and Delivery Strong verbal/written communication Schedule estimation and administration New partner engagement and relationship management Cross-group collaboration Contract negotiation	2. *Oh, well, if Steve says he has strong verbal/ written communication, it must be true! Unless you have just oodles of space and nothing to do with them, I'd suggest leaving off these "soft skills," since they're completely subjective.*
Employment **Microsoft Corporation**. Redmond, WA (2007–2010) Principal Program Manager, Microsoft Windows ■ Managed release cycle of shell components.	3. *Steve's bullets are, by and large, responsibilities. The difference is in stating the outcome. "Managed release cycle and reduced alpha-to-market time by 23%"—now that's an accomplishment!*

■ Improved UI and refocused team on simplified components. Ran focus groups and customer service feedback panels. ■ Partnered with Office and File System team to integrate components. ■ Defined strategy for team and presented memos to senior management.	
Net Systems. Pittsburgh, PA (2001–2007) Director, Information Technology ■ Led team of 30 in transition from old to new architecture, which is based off Linux kernel and the FXO protocol. The new service was more secure and more reliable but significantly more cumbersome to use. Plan was designed in one week and executed over the course of three weeks. ■ Implemented performance evaluation and rolled out process across 400-person company. ■ Oversaw cross-functional team of developers, testers, and client managers. Supervised projects and set technical direction. Motivated and inspired team, and ensured morale was high.	4. *These bullets are a bit closer to accomplishments, but could still stand to demonstrate the results in a quantifiable way a bit better.* 5. *The major problem with these bullets is that it's hard to see the relationship between what Steve did and program management. Assuming that's his chosen career path, he could probably pick accomplishments that are a bit more relevant.* 6. *Finally, the first bullet is a bit lengthy and offers a lot of extraneous information.*
Net Systems. Pittsburgh, PA (1996–2001) Senior Administrator, Information Technology ■ Managed network of 1,000 computers to reduce power usage and maintain maximum uptime.	7. *Almost without exception these bullets are responsibilities. They should be accomplishments.* 8. *The other major issue is that the responsibilities are not terribly relevant*

(continued)

(Résumé B continued)

■ Monitored two data centers using remote access technology. ■ Analyzed and optimized performance using various profiling tools. ■ Fixed crashes as they occurred on Windows operating system. ■ Oversaw upgrade from Windows 95 up through Windows 2000. Monitored system to ensure there were no service interruptions.	*to his career. Does anyone care about his fixing computers? No. He'd do better to list just the most impressive stuff, and back it up with concrete data about uptime, power usage changes, etc.*
Education **Washington University**, Dec 2001 Bachelor of Science, Computer Science	
Awards ■ Recipient of Five Microsoft "Ship It"s ■ Dean's List, 1995 ■ Won Microsoft Gold Star Award: 2008, 2009, 2010 ■ Honorable mention, West Coast Hackathon. 2003 ■ Microsoft Innovation Award: 2008 ■ Recognized for Contribution to Microsoft SQL Server. 2003.	*9. Well, now this is unfortunate. Finally we're at the bottom of his résumé, reading very carefully, and we discover that Steve's won some pretty impressive awards. Steve should cut the list's interesting awards (Ship Its, Recognitions, Dean's List, etc) and just list the Gold Star and Innovation Award.* *10. Because not everyone will recognize those awards, Steve should explain what the awards are and, if possible, some data about the selectivity.*

Assessment

You certainly walk away from this résumé with a strong impression of the candidate, but how much of that is his résumé versus his actual experience? I'm betting that a good part of the position impression is due to the fact that he is pretty impressive. Even a bad résumé can't screw that up *that* much.

At the same time, I'm not sure he's doing himself many favors with his résumé. Steve's résumé needs to his list accomplishments better and *prove* to us why they matter.

Résumé C: Geena Roberts

Employment **Blippd**. New York, NY (2008–Present) Software Engineer ■ Reduced time to render the video by 75% by implementing prediction algorithm and delayed graphics. ■ Implemented integration with OS X Spotlight Search by creating tool that extracts metadata from saved video transcripts and provides metadata to a system-wide search database. ■ Redesigned video file format and implemented backwards compatibility for search.	1. *Geena uses a substantial, quantifiable accomplishment for the very first bullet. She kicks things off on a good note.* 2. *Though it's never easy to explain why something was hard or easy on a résumé, this candidate has done a fairly good job.* 3. *The "tangible" accomplishments are reasonably clear—we can guess as to why backwards compatibility matters.*
Microsoft Corporation. Redmond, WA (Summers 2005–2007) Software Design Engineer, Intern *Visual Studio Core (Summer 2007)*	4. *Two of the four bullets show quantifiable results. It's clear from here that she made a substantial impact on the project.*
■ Implemented a user interface for the VS open file switcher (ctrl-tab) and extended it to tool windows.	

(continued)

(Résumé C continued)

■ Created service to provide gradient across VS and VS add-ins. Optimized service by 29% by caching toolbar gradient paintbrushes. *Programmer Productivity Research Center (Summers 2005, 2006)* ■ Built app to compute similarity of all methods in a code base; reduced time from $O(n^2)$ to $O(n \log n)$, enabling processing on Windows source to complete in a mere hour, down from 40 hours. ■ Created test case generation tool which creates random XML docs from XML Schema.	5. *The first bullet is valuable in its own way—it's a highly visible feature, which speaks to her credibility.*
University of Pennsylvania, Philadelphia, PA (Fall 2005–Spring 2008) ■ Courses: Advanced Java III, Software Engineering, Operating Systems. ■ Promoted to Head TA in Fall 2006; led weekly meetings and supervised four other TAs.	6. *The important points here are the course names and the fact that she was promoted. Both items are immediately obvious.*
Education **University of Pennsylvania**, May 2008 Master of Science, Computer Science. GPA: 3.6 *Graduate Coursework:* Software Engineering; Computer Architecture; Algorithms; Artificial Intelligence; Computational Theory **University of Pennsylvania**, May 2006 Bachelor of Science, Computer Science. GPA: 3.3	
Undergraduate Coursework: Operating Systems; Databases; Algorithms; Programming Languages; Computer Architecture.	

Projects **Multiuser Drawing Tool** (2007). Electronic classroom where multiple users can view and simultaneously draw on a "chalkboard" with each person's edits synchronized. C++, MFC.	*7. Geena's projects show the right amount of detail. Not too much, not too little. She is maximizing the odds that people read this section.*
Synchronized Calendar (2006–2007). Desktop calendar with globally shared calendars, allowing users to schedule meetings with other users. Calendars automatically synchronized with centralized SQL server. C#.NET, SQL, XML. *Awarded Third Prize in Computer Science Senior Design Projects.*	
Operating System (2006). UNIX-style OS with scheduler, file system, text editor and calculator. C.	
Skills ■ **Languages**: C++; C; Java; Objective-C; C#.NET; SQL; JavaScript; XSLT; XML (XSD) Schema ■ **Software**: Visual Studio; Microsoft SQL Server; Eclipse; XCode; Interface Builder	*8. Geena has kept her list of languages relatively confined. She doesn't waste time with listing things like Office and Windows, and mentions only those skills relevant to her career path.*

Assessment

Though no résumé is perfect, this one is pretty darn good. Almost all of her bullets are accomplishments, and she doesn't waste time talking about her job in generalities. Many of her accomplishments have measurable impacts.

Parting Words

Truthfully, getting your résumé into the "pretty good" stage is not that hard. Most résumés that I see fail in one of three ways:

1. **Too big**. Having a multipage résumé does not make you look more experienced—it just makes you look less concise. You should keep your résumé to one page if you have less than 10 years of experience, and two pages if you have more. You really don't need more space than that—it won't win you any favors.

2. **Too bulky**. Giant paragraphs of text scare people into just tossing your résumé in the trash. It's hard to understand when it's a product, or even a field, you don't know anything about. Use bullets to describe your accomplishments, and keep each bullet to just one to two lines.

3. **Too boring**. Recruiters are not terribly interested in what your responsibilities were. That just says what you were told to do; we want to know what you actually did. Focus on your biggest accomplishments, and quantify them as well as you can.

If you just avoid doing these three things, yours will be better than 75 percent of the résumés out there. Going the rest of the way is about tailoring your résumé to the position and explaining the impact for your work in the most favorable light possible.

Additional Resources

Please visit www.careercup.com for résumé samples and templates.

Chapter 6

Cover Letters and References

Back in the days of typewriters and snail mail, cover letters were nearly as widespread as résumés. Candidates dutifully banged out a custom note, affixed their résumé, and sent them off in a stamped and sealed envelope.

With virtually all résumés submitted electronically nowadays, cover letters are often optional. However, if you are contacting a recruiter or hiring manager to submit your résumé, your e-mail *is* your cover letter and should adhere to the standard cover letter format.

Your cover letter is a key marketing document; a strong cover letter will make someone open up your résumé to learn more.

Why a Cover Letter?

Cover letters serve two purposes. First, they enable a recruiter to quickly glance at a document to see if you match the position's requirements. Second, they allow the company to ask for a writing sample, without directly asking for it.

Why isn't your résumé good enough? Your résumé is a list of accomplishments broken down by job. Your biggest accomplishments may have to do with building a team to create a new feature, or resolving an issue with a major supplier. That lets the recruiter know that you can accomplish great things, but it doesn't necessarily inform her of your specific, relevant skills. She may be looking for data modeling, or statistical analysis, or something more "warm and fuzzy" like strong management skills.

Your résumé lets her know that you can get things done; your cover letter demonstrates your relevance to the job. Essentially, it's a teaser. It's a way to say, "I have what you're looking for, now open my résumé to see what I've accomplished."

Additionally, in writing-heavy roles, your cover letter is a way for the company to see your writing skills. Why not just come out and ask for a writing sample? Well, first, there's no reason to have you provide a make-believe business writing sample, as though you were some second grader writing a letter to the president. Second, it allows you to manufacture it too much. They want to see how you write "in the wild." You'd take extra special care to write well if you knew they were examining your every word. (And now, hopefully, you will.)

The Three Types of Cover Letter

Whether your cover letter is solicited, unsolicited, or "broadcasted," it will follow a similar format and will have similar goals. Your goal is still to excite the reader enough that he puts down your cover letter and picks up your résumé—and, hopefully, the phone. The difference lies in the degree to which the cover letter can be targeted.

Solicited Cover Letter

Most cover letters are solicited; that is, the cover letter is responding to a specific job opening advertised online, on your campus, or anywhere else. The job opening likely lists specific skills or backgrounds desired, and you need to appeal to those specific attributes. Your cover letter should explain exactly how you match those qualities, and should provide evidence using your prior experience.

"If you don't exactly match every requirement, don't let that stop you," says Matt, a former Apple recruiter. "Sometimes ads are written by recruiters or managers who don't understand that the combination of skills they want is impossible or very unlikely. Or sometimes you have other skills that may compensate for your weaknesses."

Unsolicited Cover Letter/Cold Call Letter

An unsolicited cover letter taps the hidden job market by contacting recruiters about positions that may not be advertised. Obviously, getting a job through these means is more challenging, but not at all impossible. Sometimes positions are created only when a sufficiently good candidate comes along, as is often the case with start-ups. Or other times, a friend inside the company might be able to tip you off to a new opening that has only been advertised internally.

Either way, your approach is the same: you need to identify what you think the company would want and match that. You can often extrapolate the company's needs from looking at the company's other job ads, or from looking at ads for the equivalent job at other companies.

If you think this approach seems hard, you're right. But the good news is that you will have substantially less competition if you pursue it.

Broadcast Letter

While all cover letters should be tailored, sometimes you have no choice but to create a general cover letter. This is often the case when using online job boards. The job board might encourage you to post a cover letter along with your résumé.

What to do? You should be as specific as possible, while not excluding yourself from any desired positions. If you're looking for a sales or customer support role, emphasize the skills that those positions have in common (communication, etc.).

Recruiters won't expect your cover letter to be very specific but will look at it for a quick list of your accomplishments and skill set, so make sure to really emphasize what you've achieved in your career.

The Structure

Cover letters can be so regimented that they remind me of madlibs:

"Name a skill set." Design.
"OK, now, prove that you have it." I've done design for three Fortune 500 companies, including logos, business cards, and stationery.

Yawn. But at least the structure makes it easy to write a cover letter. You don't need to be creative or even a beautiful writer to write a powerful cover letter. You just need to be able to communicate your thoughts clearly and succinctly.

A cover letter should roughly match the following template:

Dear [Recruiter or Hiring Manager's Name]:

I am interested in the [job title] advertised on [web site or other source]. With a strong background in [list of tangible skills], and [number of] years of experience in [area], I am confident that I can [general problem you can solve].

My qualifications include the following:

- **[Desired Qualification #1]:** [Proof that you have qualification #1]
- **[Desired Qualification #2]:** [Proof that you have qualification #2]
- **[Desired Qualification #3]:** [Proof that you have qualification #3]
- **[Desired Qualification #4]:** [Proof that you have qualification #4]

I would love to discuss this opportunity further. I will follow up within a [time frame] to confirm that my application was received, and to schedule a time to talk further.

Sincerely,

[Your Name]

While this letter certainly won't win any awards for prose or creativity, it's short, concise, and gets the point across: that you match the employer's needs and that you can perform the job effectively.

Many candidates shy away from using bullets in "business" writing—don't! In cover letters, as in business, you don't have to be—and *shouldn't* be—William Shakespeare; you just need to communicate clearly and effectively.

Five Traits of a Strong Cover Letter

A cover letter is not a chance to tell your life story, nor is it a chance for you to list every accomplishment you've ever had. A cover letter should introduce you, demonstrate how your background matches the job description, and state your interest in the position.

When writing yours, keep these five suggestions in mind.

1. Tailored

Recruiters are busy and, frankly, often just looking for an excuse to toss your application in the trash. One down, a few hundred to go.

Of course, they want to hire, too—their job depends on it. Their job description will tell you what they're looking for; it's up to you to show that you match it as closely as possible. If they say they want a highly quantitative marketer, then you must address that in your response.

Be wary of simply modifying an existing cover letter for a new position. The reason is that it can be tempting to leave in lines that are arguably important in general, but perhaps not as relevant to this specific position. People have a funny tendency to get attached to what they write and not want to remove parts of it.

Ideally, you should write a fresh cover letter for each application. If you won't do that, though, be sure to keep one finger on the "delete" key. It'll come in handy on any good cover letter.

What If There Is No Job Description?

In cases where there is no job description to be found, then you'll need to guess at the preferred skill set. If it's a software engineering job, try to find out what languages or technologies the team uses. For a job that's heavy on communication, call attention to your public speaking skills.

You can also track down other job ads, both from similar positions with the same company and from the same position at other companies. Look for similarities. If you find that the company always looks for someone with a particular background or that one skill is highly in demand for your position at other companies, then you can safely assume that this position will desire it, too.

2. Supported with Evidence

Anyone can say that they are hardworking, or have strong communication skills; not everyone can prove it. Use your education, work experience, and accomplishments to show the recruiter that you have the skills they need.

As with your résumé, accomplishments, especially when quantified, carry more weight than any vague discussion of your background:

> I have strong public speaking skills, a skill which was developed through four years of college Speech & Debate Team. In my final year on the team, I placed second in the state-wide Impromptu Speaking category.

3. Structured and Concise

Ever had a teammate who just rambled on and on in meetings? It's not very much fun. So why make your cover letter like that?

Your cover letter should show that you can communicate in a concise and structured way. All you need is three or four short paragraphs that clearly address the company's needs.

And remember, when people say that cover letters should be only one page, they don't mean one *full* page. Babbling is not rewarded.

4. Simple, Direct Writing

Though he may be the most acclaimed writer of all time, Shakespeare would make an awful business writer. Subtle, hidden meanings that high school sophomores need to re-read six times to even vaguely comprehend—give me a break!

If you think I'm joking, check out this sentence I saw on a cover letter:

> In my quest to embrace new opportunities and challenges, I am riveted by the chance to embark on a new path where I can utilize to the fullest extent my immense technical comprehension and where my dedication to personal excellence may thrive.

I suppose this candidate was trying to demonstrate his expansive vocabulary, but no one would be impressed by this.

You should write to communicate, not to impress. Use short, familiar words, and get to the point.

5. Professional

As a cover letter is often the best and only writing example a company has, being professional and using correct spelling and grammar is extremely important. You should proofread your own letter multiple times, and give it to a trusted friend to review as well.

Additionally, you should address the letter to the individual, if you know his or her name. If you do not know the recipient's name, never assume a gender. Who would do this? Lots of people, it turns out.

One start-up founder discovered this firsthand when she posted a job opening for her new company. The ad lacked her name, but mentioned that her background included a PhD in electrical engineering. Over 70 percent of applicants chose to address the recipient of the cover letter as "Dear Sir" instead of a more gender neutral opener.

Don't make this mistake. HR departments are awfully touchy these days about sexism.

An A+ Cover Letter

Want to move away from the boilerplate cover letter? Check out this A+ cover letter:

Dear Ms. Johnson,

I would like to request your consideration for the position of iPhone Game Developer, which I saw advertised on CareerCup.com.

I was particularly excited to see an opening within the Swords team, as this is one of what I consider to be the most addictive games. I've nearly uninstalled it from my phone but, well, I just couldn't. While the game play is fantastic as a whole, I've been particularly impressed with how the game leverages the iPhone features to implement realistic collisions.

When I picked up the job description, I knew that not only was the position a perfect match for my interests, but I was perfect match for its requirements. I have over three years of experience with writing mobile games, and pride myself on having an artistic eye despite being "just" a developer. I would love the opportunity to utilize both the artistic and the technical aspects of my brain. My games have been shipped to three mobile platforms, with over 100,000 downloads on the iPhone itself.

Additionally, I place high value on the long-term maintainability of a code base, and have implemented systems at my previous company to improve code quality. Most notably, I restructured our coding cycle to match industry best standards. Gone were the days of bang-it-out; developers needed to write design documents for any external APIs and have them peer reviewed by at least two people. All source must be code reviewed before being checked in. Bugs at the "critical" level dropped 19 percent with the implementation of this new system.

I think that Swords and I could have a wonderful working relationship; we're compatible down to the last little detail.

I look forward to talking with you more about this opportunity. Please contact me at 206-555-9323. Thank you for your consideration.

Sincerely,

Gayle Laakmann

What makes this cover letter so fantastic is that it shows a bit of character while also demonstrating one's relevant skills (that were presumably mentioned in the job description). The discussion of skills is backed up with evidence, and the candidate has obviously done her research.

This is the kind of cover letter that'll make your recruiter salivate.

References

"One time I called a candidate's reference and she said that the candidate had been fired for theft—a fact the candidate had not revealed to me," recounted Matthew, a serial tech entrepreneur. "Another time I called and discovered that the reference himself had been fired months earlier. And then there was the time that the reference paused, took a deep breath, and explained to me that he's found giving bad references comes back to haunt him. He prefers to avoid that situation now, and he hoped I would *understand*. The pause before the last word was suggestive, to say the least. Oh, and I can't forget my favorite: I once called a reference only to notice that her voice sounded remarkably similar to the candidate's. I called back later for some additional 'clarification,' only to get redirected to the candidate's own voicemail."

While these candidates acted extremely foolish, they made the same mistakes many candidates make. They failed to demonstrate honesty and integrity, and they did not communicate effectively with the reference about her ability to provide a strong reference or any reference at all.

Who Makes a Strong Reference?

You do not need to provide the same references for every job. In fact, if you're applying for a variety of roles, you should vary your references, depending on the skills required.

A strong reference will fit all of the following criteria:

- **Knowledge of your work.** A strong reference will be one who has worked directly with you for at least six months, if not several years, and who can speak in-depth about your skills and accomplishments. And, of course, this should be someone who liked you.
- **Articulate.** You've worked with your references long enough (hopefully) to know if they communicate well. If they sound ditzy or speak with terrible grammar, they may not inspire confidence when they speak about your intelligence. You want someone who can elaborate just the right amount and can cite concrete examples.
- **Positive communicator.** Not everyone who likes you will be able to speak well of you. Some people are just too negative, while others may not be able to communicate clearly. John, a Microsoft employee looking to switch careers, opted to not have his manager give his review, turning instead to his manager's manager. "My direct manager liked me, but he was a poor communicator—one of those guys who almost never seemed pleased, even when he was. His manager, on the other hand, knew my work very well, and was generally more prone to positive reassurance. The choice was a no-brainer."
- **Understands the desired position.** A reference who understands the position will be able to more effectively communicate your ability to fulfill the responsibilities.
- **Available and eager.** When a reference can't spare the time to talk to a prospective employer, it can seem as though the reference isn't sure about your skills. Make sure that your reference is happy to do this favor for you, and don't burden him any more than necessary.

When you select your references, think about what skills are most important to a new position. Your references could come from a number of sources, including peers, mentors, vendors, or even customers. Your most recent supervisor is often the best reference if you've left the company and did so on good terms. In fact, not offering this person as a reference will often raise red flags.

No matter how many references you list, the company may do its own digging. After all, everyone can come up with three good references; the true test is whether nonsolicited references also turn up positive.

How to Make Good References Great

Where do bad references come from? From candidates who don't spend time on their references. References should be prepped for each and every position. Who will be contacting them, and what will they want to know? The more prepared the reference is, the more positive she will be. Trust me—there's nothing worse than waking up at 8 AM to an unexpected call, only to have a stranger jabber away about skills for some job at some company you know nothing about.

Following the steps below will ensure you a much stronger reference, and will earn the appreciation of everyone involved as well.

1. **Ask permission.** Every time you distribute a reference's name, you need to ask the reference's permission and confirm the contact information. The reference might have moved on, or he might simply be traveling and prefer to be contacted on his personal phone or e-mail.

2. **Describe the position.** Tell your reference about the position. Why do you want it? What are your career goals? Why do you think you would be a great match?

3. **Refresh their memory.** Your reference might have forgotten about some of your greatest accomplishments. Remind her of what your responsibilities were, what your accomplishments were, how you accomplished them, and

what your greatest challenges were. At a minimum, if your reference would be expected to know about some of your accomplishments listed on your résumé, make sure to discuss the details of these with her.

4. **Update them.** If you've taken any additional courses or had any significant experiences, describe these to your reference. These may come in handy.

5. **Suggest areas to emphasize.** While you can *never* ask your reference to lie, offering suggestions on areas to stress is acceptable and even helpful. If you want to make sure that the caller knows that you're a strong negotiator, you can mention this to your contact. They'll appreciate the guidance—I know I would.

6. **Discuss the bad stuff.** Your reference will almost surely be asked for your weaknesses or for examples of mistakes you've made. Although this can be awkward to discuss, it's better to do so now than for your reference to have to make something up on the spot. You can mention a few different topics, and let her decide what to discuss.

7. **Follow up.** Thank your reference for his assistance, and make sure to follow up with him about what happens.

This conversation should ideally happen over the phone. If so, you should follow up with an e-mail reiterating the major topics, and reminding your reference of the company name and position.

Problems with References: What Can Go Wrong

If you seem to lose the job offer just past the reference-checking stage, your references may (or may not) be the culprit. How will you ever know? I'll leave it to you to analyze the ethics of this, but some candidates have engaged friends to call references and investigate these concerns.

A more direct approach is to just ask your references to run them through what they've been asked, and what their responses have been. Encourage them to be open about the negative things as well, because, after all, a 100 percent positive review is never credible.

If you still can't figure it out, ask yourself these questions:

- **Do your references have any major black marks themselves?** If they've been fired or significantly demoted, they may not offer a ton of credibility.
- **Are your references effective communicators?** When you challenged their positions on a matter, were you able to understand their reasoning?
- **Do your references communicate in a positive way?** Think back to your reviews. Did they focus on the positive or the negative?
- **Are they knowledgeable about your prior projects?** They may just need a refresher course on what you accomplished under them, or they may need to be yanked completely.
- **Are they familiar with what you're doing now?** If you've lost touch with your references, invite them to grab coffee with you. Discuss what they're working on—and what you're doing.

Bad references can be caused by many things. If you suspect a contact is offering a negative review, you may want to play it safe and remove him entirely.

What If Your Bad Reference Is Your Former Boss?

If you have personal differences with your current boss, this will likely not present an issue. A prospective company should never call your current company without your permission.

But what if you've left your old company and your hopefully future company insists on speaking to your former boss? You have many options, and none of them involve asking someone to lie. (Never, ever ask a reference to lie. Do you really want someone to think of you as dishonest right before they talk about your weaknesses?)

First, you should call your old manager and discuss your concerns up front. Explain what you think your strengths were, and be blunt about your weaknesses. Without making excuses for yourself, tell her why these presented themselves in such a negative way, and how you've been working on them. What sort of progress have you made? This will deemphasize the weakness, and you may even be able to suggest less harmful vocabulary (such as "can occasionally get heated" instead of "has an angry temper").

Second, if the review is particularly bad (such as being fired for exposing company secrets), you need to be up front about this with the new HR department. It's better that they hear it from you, rather than being caught off-guard by your ex-manager.

Finally, you may be able to offer additional references in certain cases to compensate for a poor reference. Audrey, a technical sales representative, quit her job after being assigned a manager who frequently yelled at his employees for even small mistakes. She had no chance of improving this review. Instead, she explained the situation to her prospective employer and offered contact information for three former teammates. They would not only corroborate her story, but they would also offer a strong reference for her. She got the job.

Your Questions Answered

New Form, Same Great Content

Dear Gayle,

I've tried to write a cover letter multiple times, but each time I feel like I'm just turning my résumé into prose. Is this normal? And is it OK?

~R. T.

Dear R. T.,

Normal? Yes. OK? Maybe.

Many people hit the same issue, so if you do, it's not the end of the world. A good part of the reason for a cover letter is to check that you can write. Employers can check your spelling, grammar, and structure just about as well in this boring, regurgitated form.

However, it may be a missed opportunity to give your employer more information than they can read on your résumé. Your goal here is to prove that you have the desired skills. You can do that using accomplishments (which will likely be repeated on your résumé), or by using slightly softer evidence. For example, to prove that you understand object-oriented design coding, you can say something like this:

Object-Oriented Design: I taught a three-course sequence to the company's developers on design patterns, which my manager said was "instrumental in raising the quality of our company's code."
Or:

Detail Oriented: I was the "go to" person on any design doc, not only because I understood the company's technology at a broad level, but also because I had a knack for picking up on issues that were otherwise overlooked.

Writing a cover letter like this is certainly much harder, but when you start getting calls that your competing candidates don't, you'll be thankful.

~Gayle

Full Disclosure

Dear Gayle,

Should I tell my manager that I'm looking for a new job? I'm coming to the end of a rotation program, so my leaving shouldn't be a complete surprise, but it's still not exactly encouraged.

I'm worried that prospective employers will contact my manager for a reference, and I wouldn't want him to find out the wrong way.

~F. S.

Dear F. S.,

There's no need to tell your manager. Your prospective companies should not contact any references without your explicit permission. Just to make extra sure, though, you should let the prospective company know the situation. It's quite normal—in fact, the norm—for people to not tell their manager until they've accepted the new offer.

However, perhaps you have some reason to believe your manager stands a very good chance of finding out. If, for example, you know that your manager has a close friend at the companies or teams you're applying, I wouldn't count on this friend's discretion. In this case, given that your leaving is not totally unexpected, discussing the situation with your manager might be wise.

What's the worst he can do, fire you?

~Gayle

Dear Gayle,

After college, I founded my own business. We did OK for a little while and I hired a few people, but things took a turn for the worse.

Anyway, here I am, looking for work. Employers want to check references, but I've never had a boss. Who should I give?

~T. R.

Dear T. R.,

Former employees, clients, investors, and partners all make great references, and each have their pros and cons.

Investors make great references. They may not know you quite as well as a manager would in most jobs, but they're the closest thing you have to a "boss."

Your employees will know you extremely well, but with the power dynamic (even if it shouldn't be an issue), employers may not trust that they're being fully honest.

Clients and partners can also be useful. They'll know certain aspects of you quite well, and won't have much reason to be misleading like your employees might.

The best thing to do, really, is to explain the situation to the employer. Ask your recruiter which type would be the most valuable, and then track down the relevant references. There's no reason you shouldn't check with your recruiter about logistical questions like this.

Remember, though, that just because you didn't list a particular client doesn't mean your recruiter won't track them down. A good reference checker, in fact, will do more than just check off a preapproved list.

~Gayle

Additional Resources

Please visit www.careercup.com for sample cover letters and other resources.

Chapter 7

Interview Prep
and Overview

Think you've got it rough? Look at it from the company's perspective. A good hire is incredibly valuable, bad hires are even more costly, and interviews are a not-terribly-cheap way to cut their costs.

A typical Microsoft on-site interview for an entry-level software engineer costs the company over $1,000 in plane flights, hotels, and "man-hours." Multiply that by the number of candidates who don't get hired and you're looking at over $10,000 just for the interviews. We haven't even taken into account the paperwork process, signing bonuses, relocation, and all the recruiter overhead it takes to manage this process.

Hire someone bad and the company's costs go up even more. Not only did the company waste money on this person's salary, but the employee was likely a distraction to their team as well. Then—worst of all—in the United States, the company faces the risk of wrongful termination lawsuits. No wonder companies give so many interviews!

In the end, a company wants people who "get things done," and résumé screening and interviews are a way to analyze you from this perspective. It wants people who are more than just smart; it wants

108

people who motivate those around them, who set lofty goals and accomplish them, who act ethically and honestly.

While these are largely "fundamental" attributes of you or your background, the way that you communicate and respond to questions determines how a company reads such attributes. The eager candidate can—and should—prepare for the interview to help them put the best foot forward.

What Are Tech Companies Looking For?

Passion. Creativity. Initiative. Intelligence. And a "getting things done" attitude.

Tech companies operate a bit differently from the rest of corporate America. They don't wear suits. Few employees arrive much before 10 AM, due in part to horrendous traffic in tech hubs like Seattle and Silicon Valley. Post-lunch (or midmorning, or midafternoon) foosball and ping-pong games are standard.

They pride themselves on their funky and innovative culture, and they want people who will fit into this. "You have to prove why you are there, and that you *know* you fit within their community, that you enjoy the lifestyle," said Andre, a (successful) Apple candidate. "The moment my interviewer said, 'We are very informal' I took off my tie."

- **Passion for technology.** Passion for technology can be shown through your coursework, but it doesn't end there. Do you read tech news sources? Do you use technology in your day-to-day life (beyond just e-mail and basic web browsing)? Are you interested in finding new ways to leverage or improve technology?
- **Passion for the company.** Do you know the company's products? Do you use them? Why or why not? What would you improve?

- **Creativity.** When asked to design something from scratch, can you brainstorm lots of features you'd want? When you're asking to solve a problem, do you think outside the box and push back on assumptions or constraints?
- **Initiative.** How have you gone above and beyond? Have you started a blog? A business? Organized a charity auction? Remember that initiative might be something as nontraditional as putting on a photography show.
- **Getting things done.** Regardless of where the idea came from, do you have a demonstrated ability to accomplish great things? Think beyond just your academic or professional work: what have you done outside of work?
- **Intelligence.** Your GPA can be one show of intelligence, but people with GPAs well below a 3.0/4.0 can and do get hired at the best tech companies. Intelligence can be "tested" through problem-solving questions, or hinted at through your résumé.

At the end of the day, it comes down to this: can you communicate how you can help the company? Passion, creativity, initiative, intelligence, and a "getting things done" attitude are all signals of that.

How to Prepare

For at least the less technical aspects of an interview, preparation comes in three parts. You need to be able to answer questions about your prior work with illustrative examples. You need to understand the company so that you can tell your interviewer why you want to work there and what you'll add. And, finally, you need to be able to ask interesting questions to your interviewer that demonstrate your research and interest.

Résumé and Experience Prep

Regardless of the position or company, almost every interview will include some discussion of your résumé. The more "hard skills" that a position requires, the less focus there will be on the résumé/experience discussion—but there will always be some.

Practice Your Pitch

For each job or position, practice stating a short blurb explaining what your role was and what you accomplished. Practice two blurbs: one that would be understandable from those in your field, and one that's understandable for nonspecialists. Stay light on the details and let the interview probe as necessary.

Pay special attention to the pitches for your most recent role, as they're the most relevant. You could even consider recording this pitch and playing it back to yourself—do you mumble during certain parts? Friends can also be useful here. Where do they think you are weakest and strongest?

Review Your Résumé

From past projects to your foreign or programming languages, anything on your résumé is fair game. If you claim that you're fluent in German, be prepared for a company to verify this. Tech companies are extremely international, and it's not hard to find someone who speaks a language.

The day before your interview, pick up your résumé and explain each bullet out loud, just as you would if your interviewer asks, "What did you mean by this line?" Make sure you can explain the "what, how, and why."

Preparation Grid

Imagine your interviewer throws you the following question: "Tell me about a time when you had a difficult situation with a coworker." Could you answer it? Possibly. Now imagine he asks you to pick a time from a specific project that you worked on three years ago. You *know* you've experienced difficult times, so why is it so hard to think of one? Because that's just not the way our brain works.

That's why it's so important to create a preparation grid. The preparation grid allows you to construct answers in advance to each major type of question for each project or role you've had. The columns represent each project, and the rows represent the most common behavioral question. If you are applying for an engineering role, the rows should instead be the common technical questions, such as the hardest bug or biggest algorithm challenge.

	Advertising Engine	Encryption
Most Challenging	Balancing time vs. cost trade-off	Replacing bottom layer of system
What You Learned	Too much design is unrealistic	Eng. goals can conflict with mktg.
Influencing Someone	Senior mgmt. to refocus project	Changing triage system
Conflict	Bob had vested interest in status quo	Dealing with alleged experts
Mistake	Didn't gather enough support in advance	Not considering all dependencies

Fill each cell with a story that would respond to the question. When you fill in your grid, limit each story to just a few key words—this will make it easier to recall. If you do a phone interview, consider having the preparation grid in front of you.

You can download a fresh copy of the preparation grid from www.careercup.com.

Do Your Homework

Recruiting is expensive, and companies want to know that you're excited about the job. They hate having a candidate reject their offer almost as much as candidates hate getting rejected. Moreover, enthusiastic candidates are more likely to work hard at a job and stay at the company. Companies look for enthusiasm, and researching the company, position, and people is one way to prove that.

Additionally, by doing this research, you'll be able to forge stronger connections with your interviewers, learn more in the process, and sometimes even predict interview questions.

"Before my Amazon interview, I bought a Kindle," Dave, a (now) Amazon employee, said. "It was expensive, but I needed that job badly. I also explored s3, ec2, and basically every Amazon product I could get my hands on. I was interviewing with a back-end team, but people move around—I knew that my interviewers had likely worked on other teams in the past. And I was right. Several of my interviewers had worked on Kindle and other products, and I was able to ask informed questions about their teams. Needless to say, they were impressed."

Company

Company research starts with the basics: what do they make, how do they make it, and how do they make money? These answers sometimes appear more straightforward than they really are. Amazon, for instance, makes money by reselling products at a small profit. The interesting question is how: how are they able to sell so many things? By having some of the best distribution systems and infrastructure out there!

- **News.** Stay on top of the latest news about a company, especially if you're interviewing for a nontechnical role.

The more important "current events" are to your role, the more important it is for you to know about this for your interview. Twitter can be a great source for "unfiltered" company news if you search what other users are saying. The corporate blog can also be valuable, but keep in mind that blogs are usually more of a "PR machine" than anything else.

- **Competitors.** Not only are competitors likely to have similar problems, but a competitor's success is the company's problem. Research who the competitors are, as well as why: in what ways is one company doing better than another? Why are they doing better?

- **Current and Former Employees.** Use Twitter, Facebook, or your friends network to reach out to current and former employees. They may be able to share with you some insights about the company, and, if you're lucky, offer some interview tips.

- **Culture.** Companies with a particularly strong culture are likely to select for culture fit, and are likely to openly discuss their culture. Zappos.com, for instance, is known for having a very fun and quirky culture. Don't be surprised if they ask you for a time when you broke the rules, or to invent a new type of pizza topping. Zappos's interview questions reflect their weirdness, and they will look to see if you're weird enough to fit in.

Interviewer Research

If you're given the name of your interviewer, you can use this to your advantage. Find her Twitter, Facebook, or LinkedIn account to discover her interests, or sometimes even specific projects that she's worked on. This will give you a clue as to what sorts of questions to ask, or how to drive the discussion.

Prepare Questions

At either the beginning or end of each question, your interviewer will give you a chance to ask questions. The quality of your questions will be a factor, whether subconsciously or consciously, in his decision. Ask open-ended questions that the person you're interviewing with can tackle.

While some questions may come to you at the time (which is great), you can—and should—prepare 10 to 15 questions in advance. This will ensure that you have at least a few questions to ask every interviewer. *Tip:* You will usually be allowed to bring a "résumé notebook" with a pad of paper into your interview. You can jot down questions in advance there and refer to it.

Consider questions from the following three categories:

1. **Genuine questions.** These are the questions you actually want to know the answers to. These questions might be:
   - "How much of your day do you spend coding?" (if you're an engineering candidate)
   - "How many people are on the team? What's the breakdown of different positions?"
   - "What are the biggest issues facing the team?"
   - "How does the decision process work? Who makes the final call? Who drives the decisions?"

2. **Insightful questions.** These questions show that you've thought deeply about the issues facing the team or company. Research you do in advance will come in handy here. For example:
   - "Office has been aggressively pursuing an online strategy. Is this a play at the consumer market to protect Microsoft from Google? Or is there a role in the business market as well, since that's where Microsoft makes most of its money?"

- "Why did Google opt to use an open protocol for this product? Is it mainly a PR move, or are there actually technology advantages? What sort of limitations is Google usually concerned with when leveraging open source?"

3. **Passion questions.** Passion questions are designed to show you as someone who is excited about technology, about the company, or about learning. These questions include:

- "Though I don't have a coding background, I love learning how software is implemented. As an employee, what sorts of resources are there to do this?"
- "I'm not familiar with the technology you mentioned earlier. Could you tell me a bit about it?"
- "Thinking back to people who have had this job in the past, what separates the successful person from the unsuccessful?"

Because you are expected to do research prior to your interview, you should avoid asking questions that could have been easily looked up.

Additionally, remember that you will likely interview with HR, a manager, and teammates as well. What perspective can they each offer about the company?

Working with Your Recruiter

Your recruiter serves as your advocate during the recruiting process. He *wants* you to do well—after all, his performance evaluation is largely determined by the quantity and quality of candidates he brings in. He's unlikely to be making the final "hire/no hire" decision, but he can be a voice that fights for you.

No one knows this better than Ravi. Ravi was applying for a position at Microsoft—his dream job. Ravi breezed through the on-campus interviews at his college and was flown out to Redmond, Washington, for five interviews with two different teams. He met with his recruiter at the end of the day, who thanked him very much for his time and scooted him out the door. He left the rainy city with no offer in hand. A week later, he started sweating—why hadn't she called? Finally, two weeks after his interview, he learned the bad news: though he had done well, she said, neither team would be moving forward at this time. Ah, the generic words every candidate hates to hear!

Normally, that would be that. However, instead of shutting the door on him (and his dream job), she invited him to return to Seattle for another set of interviews. He flew out again, completed another five interviews, and again, days passed with no word. Finally, she called Ravi: "Neither team will be moving forward at this time, but we have a different team that would like to speak with you." Two phone interviews later, and bam! He got the offer and went on to have the best summer of his life.

Why was Ravi special? He and his recruiter clicked, and she believed in him. She recognized that interviews are a bit random and take some practice. She was willing to give him a second—and then third—chance.

Your goal, during a recruiting process, is to build a connection with your recruiter like Ravi did. Though they may not have the hire/no hire decision, they can and do fight for you to get an offer—or not.

Getting the Recruiter on Your Side

Simply by respecting the recruiter's role, you're off to a great start. Far too many candidates see recruiters as just a minion in the recruiting process who is there to do their bidding.

- **Be polite.** Always show your recruiter politeness and courtesy. Follow up with him, but don't pester him. Respect that he's busy and works with many candidates.

- **Use good grammar and spelling.** Using correct grammar and spelling when e-mailing your recruiter will show professionalism. Minor grammatical mistakes will probably be forgiven, especially for international candidates, but "text messaging style" abbreviations are not acceptable. Never write your recruiter with language like, "wat time is d interview." Make spell check and grammar check your friends.

- **Ask questions.** Ask the recruiter questions about the company, the position, and so on. Make sure that these questions don't have easily discoverable answers online. By asking insightful questions, you show that you're passionate about the company—and about learning.

- **Seek their advice.** Though the recruiter may not be an expert in finance, engineering, marketing, or whatever position you're applying for, she's probably seen a lot more interviews than you have. Seek the recruiter's advice about what skill sets are more important, how to prepare for the interview, and the like. Even if she can't answer your questions, she'll appreciate that you respect her opinion enough to ask.

Communication and Behavior

"I did horribly," Avi tells me. I know how this is going to go; I've had this conversation more times than I can count.

"OK, what happened? Why do you think that?"

"I can just tell. She just didn't seem happy with any of the answers I gave her." And there we have it—new candidate, new interview, same mistakes. I go on to explain to Avi his mistake: that an interviewer's unfriendliness or friendliness has much more to do with her own personality than the candidate's performance.

An interview is a window into a company; just as the interviewer is trying to look into you and discover your strengths and weaknesses, you will no doubt evaluate the interviewer as a proxy for the company. And interviewers know this.

For this reason, a good interviewer will do his best to leave you with a positive impression, regardless of your performance. He should smile, offer positive reassurance, and give you his full attention. Even if he has effectively written you off as a "no hire," you have friends and colleagues who may interact with the company down the road. Recruiting is too important to a company's future to just disregard anyone's perceptions.

Of course, there are still unfriendly interviewers. There are interviewers who push back on your responses with a condescending tone, and there are interviewers who are distracted and don't give you their full attention. They probably usually behave like that. Unless you know your interviewer from other situations (which would be inappropriate), you have no idea how to interpret his attitude.

With all that said, an interviewer's behavior is probably 80 percent his personality and 20 percent you—this is the "80/20 Rule of Body Language." That 80 percent makes it difficult to understand *why* your interviewer is acting a particular way, but that 20 percent you can leverage to put yourself in the best possible situation.

Controlling the Interview

Hopefully, you're walking into the interview with a host of stories behind you. But what if the interviewer doesn't ask the right things? If they're not headed in the direction you want, lead them there. Here's an example:

Interviewer: What was your project at Google?
Candidate: I joined just after Google acquired YouTube, and I was responsible for figuring out a plan for merging YouTube's technology with Google's. The two companies were working with some of the same basic technologies, but I needed to figure out how much—if at all—to merge them. I quickly discovered that YouTube could be made much more cost effective by leveraging

the Google Video libraries. I spent most of my time working on the video compression library, which is where I hit some of the most interesting challenges.

What do you think is the next question she'll ask? If she's at all interested, she'll probably ask you to elaborate on the challenges you faced. If she's not interested, then aren't you glad you didn't ramble?

By leading your interviewer like this, you'll be able to drive the conversation in a way that's positive for both you and your interviewer, rather than drown her in details.

Alternatively, you can be more direct and say: "I can elaborate on that if you'd like." This is a good way of skipping over details in a story that an interviewer may or may not want to hear.

Four Ways to Keep the Interviewer's Attention

I wish I could tell you that interviewers were eager to speak to you—that they open your résumé well in advance, research your projects, and maybe even check out the web site that you conveniently listed on your application. For some—especially the newly minted interviewers—this might be the case.

But, as interviewers become more experienced, their enthusiasm tends to wane. The walk over to the interview room becomes the ideal slice of time for résumé preparation. While you're diving into the nitty-gritty details of how you saved your current employer from impending doom, your interviewer is picturing the ever-growing mountain of work waiting for them. They know the importance of the interview both to you and to the company, but at the same time, they just want to be done already!

You can't really blame your interviewer (too much), but you can be proactive in detecting when they're losing focus and in bringing them back to you.

Keep an eye out for your interviewer glancing at their computer or phone. (If you're on a phone interview, look for unusual silences.) This is a sign that they're losing focus.

Don't call them on it—it won't earn you any points. Rather, try these tips:

- **Vary your speech.** Try varying the volume or tone of your speech. Speaking a bit louder or a bit quieter may be the kick needed to grab your interviewer's attention. Or, if you can show some additional passion or enthusiasm in your voice, your interviewer might absorb some of this emotion.

- **Tell a story.** Minor changes in word choice can flip your response from a bland description of what happened to a memorable story. Consider the difference between "The servers were experiencing significant downtimes during peak ordering times, which made us lose money" and "I answered the phone to hear a customer screaming at us because our web site was down. As we looked into it, we discovered this was a widespread issue that caused our department to lose about $10,000 each month." Adding action to the story will grab the listener's attention, while quantifying the impact will ground what you're saying in fact. Be careful not to go overboard, though—you don't want to drown the person in details either.

- **Talk less.** Rather than giving all the aspects of a story, consider limiting yourself to just the important facts—that is, the things that are essential to understand what you did and why it mattered. Does the interviewer need to know that the coworker in your story is French? Unless the story is about a language barrier, probably not.

- **Structure your responses.** Ever listened to someone speak and ask yourself, "Where is this story going?" Sometimes this is because the person is talking too much, but sometimes it's just due to a lack of structure. Picture your response as a set of bullets and sub-bullets—and use them while speaking! For example: "We had two major issues with this design: one, our customers are very cost-sensitive, and two, it would take too long to implement. As far as the first point, we believed that . . ." Hand gestures can help make the division between your points even clearer.

With all of this advice, remember the 80/20 Rule of Body Language. If your interviewer's attention drifts, she's probably just like that in general. Don't lose hope or get discouraged, but *do* act on it.

Projecting Confidence

Confidence is a delicate balancing game: too much confidence and you appear arrogant; too little confidence and you appear insecure. You need to find the "sweet spot"—the point where you are assertive with your own opinions, and are bold enough to take some risks, but you also listen and respect others.

Whether you have lots of confidence or little, keep in mind this advice:

- **Eye contact.** Making eye contact with your interviewer shows confidence and—short of starting a staring contest—you probably can't go overboard with this. If you are the type to stare at the desk or up in the air while trying to construct an answer, then make sure to maintain steady eye contact.
- **Match your volume.** Roughly matching your voice to your interviewer's will ensure that you speak at an appropriate volume that doesn't get read as too aggressive or too passive. Of course, don't go overboard on this—if your interviewer

is barely audible, you should just soften your voice only as much as it easily comfortable for you.

- **Don't argue (too much).** Occasionally, your interviewer might say something you disagree with—and you might even be correct. Speak up, but gently. Use wording like, "Interesting—I thought that Apple had stated they wouldn't enter this market," and then if your interviewer stands firm, "Oh, all right, I must be thinking of something else." No matter how sure you are, always remember that your interviewer thinks you're wrong. And it's your interviewer's opinion that matters.

- **Watch out for nervous habits.** Fidgeting with your watch. Chewing on pencils. Twirling your hair between your fingers. Any of these sound familiar? Nervous habits like this not only suggest that you lack confidence, but they can also be distracting or even offensive to your interviewers.

Special Interview Types

While much interview advice is broadly applicable, there is some advice that is most applicable to specific types of interviews.

The Phone Interview

Phone interviews are usually conducted early in the interview process, as a precursor to the on-site interview. Some companies may additionally use instant messenger or a document-sharing site when sending code or other text.

What to Bring

Though you'll usually be doing your phone interviews from your own home or office, make sure to have the following out in front of you:

- **Calculator.** In case you need to do quick calculations.

- **Pencil and paper.** Use this to jot down notes or potential questions to ask the interviewer.
- **Your résumé.** Your interviewer will be using your résumé to ask you questions, so it's helpful to be able to look at the exact document to know what he's reading from.
- **Computer.** Have it out in front of you in case your interviewer needs you to open up a document or reference a web site. But *keep it closed until then*. If you try to look up answers on your computer, it'll only distract you and it's unlikely to fool your interviewer.
- **Your interview prep grid.** Remember the interview prep grid we discussed earlier? A phone interview is a perfect time to have it out in front of you.
- **Notes.** It's fine to keep some reference material out in front of you, but keep it simple. If you have to read anything more than a couple of words, it's more likely to distract you than help you.

How to Do Well

- **Find a quiet place.** Dogs barking or babies crying will not only distract you from an interview, but they'll also show a lack of professionalism and responsibility on your part. Find a nice, quiet place to conduct your phone interview.
- **Avoid rescheduling (but do so if necessary).** Try not to reschedule your interview. However, if you need to, then do so! Mike, a Google candidate, was so afraid of rescheduling his interview that he ended up conducting it standing up in a maintenance closet. He did not get the offer.
- **Smile!** Even though your interviewer may not be able to see you, smiles are reflected in your voice (and psychology tests show it'll actually make you happier). And who doesn't want to work with a cheerful person?

The HR Screening Interview

The HR screening interviewer is "just" a recruiter, right? Wrong!

While the screening interview is usually performed by recruiters or another HR representative who are unlikely to deeply evaluate your technical skills, do not blow off this interview. The screening interview is the company's first impression of you and, like all first impressions, they matter!

What Is It?

The screening interview is usually performed by a recruiter or another HR representative over the phone and serves as an efficient way to determine if a candidate meets the basic requirements. The screener is essentially trying to match you against the backgrounds of those who have done well. Are you a match?

Matching this skill set is often simply a matter of educational background and work experience, but may at times delve into extra-curricular. One interviewer mentioned how she loved to hire soccer players. This seems silly (and it probably is), but she said the strongest two interns from the year before were both varsity soccer players. After all, she said, soccer players possess determination and team-work—and aren't those attributes you want in your colleagues?

The HR screen is often skipped when a candidate's background is clearly and directly relevant (for example, a Microsoft developer applying for a developer position at Google). Therefore, do *not* assume that the first interview is automatically an HR screening interview—even if it's called a "phone screen." If you are unsure, ask your interview coordinator what position your interviewer has.

What Happens?

The HR screener will likely ask questions to evaluate your character, background, and basic intelligence. Any skill-specific questions should be at a cursory level. Questions may also be designed to probe any potential red flags, such as frequent job hopping.

These interviews are usually conducted over the phone, but may also employ video chat or computer tests.

How to Do Well

In addition to the usual guidance for interviews, consider this advice:

- **Look for red flags.** A core goal of the HR screening interview is to evaluate any potential red flags on your résumé. Do you have several jobs of less than two years? Did you switch from a seemingly more prestigious company or position to a less prestigious one? Give your résumé to a friend and ask him what the weakest point on your résumé is. What would his biggest concern be if he were a recruiter?

- **Be prepared for salary questions.** Like it or not, HR screeners will often ask you for your salary requirements. They need to know if you're too expensive. Before your interview, use the Internet and your friends network to get a feel for salary ranges. If you are asked for your salary requirements, you should try to avoid giving a specific answer so as not to set your sights too low or too high. However, the interviewer may continue to press you on this question, in which case you will be prepared to give an answer.

Lunch Interviews

Almost all on-site interviews will include a mealtime interview because, frankly, they can't let you starve. Mealtime interviews also have the additional value of being a bit more social and allowing you to let down your guard. After all, companies want to know what you're like on a day-to-day basis.

Lunch (or dinner) interviews also offer you a great chance to ask a lot of questions about the company. Your interviewer is also relaxed and might offer more honest responses.

Depending on the company, your lunch interviewer may or may not ask "real" questions, and she may or may not submit feedback. Even if your interviewer does not submit feedback officially, you should still be on your best behavior—people talk.

How to Do Well

- **Don't order messy foods.** Ribs, spaghetti, and anything else likely to mark up your clothing is off-limits.
- **Take cues from the interviewer.** Order food that's in a similar price range as your interviewer. If your interviewer is talking about personal topics, like his vacation, it's probably OK for you to as well. If your interviewer is sticking to work topics, then you should, too. And, no matter how well you and your interviewer are getting along, always remember to be wary of socially sensitive topics—yes, that means no discussing your views on gun rights. Unless you're interviewing with the NRA, it's probably not appropriate.
- **Limit your liquids.** Need I say more? You don't want to be running to the bathroom constantly.
- **Check your teeth afterwards.** Though hopefully no one would reject a candidate simply because she has food in her teeth, it's still probably not the impression one wishes to make. Find a convenient time to use the restroom and check for this.

Follow-up Interviews

In rare cases, you might be scheduled for a follow-up interview after completing a full set of on-site interviews. This can happen because they have a specific concern with your application or because they didn't test something thoroughly enough, or simply because an additional manager wishes to speak with you before giving a final decision.

If this happens to you, try asking your recruiter if there's any particular focus for this interview or if it's standard procedure. He might not tell you, but it doesn't hurt to ask!

If you aren't given any specific direction for this interview, you should reflect on your last set of interviews: what do you think you did more poorly on, or were there gaps in what they asked you? This may offer one focus area, but remember that you might not be correct in your assessment. You should therefore do general prep, with just a slight focus on certain areas.

Finally, you should be prepared with two to three new questions that show additional thought or research. What you learned in your prior interviews is a great source of inspiration for your questions.

After the Interview

That unmistakable relief that you're done with your interview is soon replaced by an unmistakable anxiety about how it went. You replay the entire interview in your head: Did you do OK? Did you make any mistakes? What did the recruiter mean when he said, "We'll get in touch with you soon"? I'd tell you not to sweat it, but it probably won't do any good. Instead, let's focus on what you need to do after your interview.

The "Thank You" Note

Although post-interview thank you notes are essentially required in many interviews, they're fairly unusual in tech companies. Howard Wu, a T-Mobile and former Amazon interviewer, estimated that he received thank you notes from fewer than 10 percent of his candidates. For engineering candidates, this number is probably closer to 1 percent.

Eric, a former Amazon interviewer, joked that "for tech companies, a thank you note is like wearing a suit to the interview. It's out of place, and it looks like you're trying to compensate for something." While other people may be less negative, it's generally agreed that a thank you note won't help you. Feedback is usually submitted so quickly after your interview that you couldn't impact their decision.

However, a short note to your recruiter thanking her for coordinating your interview can certainly be nice. If you decide to send a thank you note, either to your recruiter or to an interviewer, they usually follow a format similar to the one below:

Dear John,

I wanted to thank you for your time today. I was particularly interested in the discussion we had about the upcoming scalability and power constraints that the company is expected to soon face. I've been interested in big system design for some time now, and I am eager to learn more about it.

During my time in college, I enrolled in several courses on distributed systems. My current position has offered me an excellent foundation in designing reliable software, and I've continued to pursue my interest in large system design through implementing various web automation projects during my free time.

I feel confident that I can leverage my academic, professional, and "extracurricular" experience with software development to make an impact on Google. I look forward to the opportunity to continue discussions with the company.

Thanks again,

~Gayle

This sample thank you note does several things that you should look to replicate in your own letter:

- **Specificity.** While I could have borrowed the occasional sentence from a prior thank you note, the references to a specific discussion make it impossible for it to be completely cut-and-paste.
- **Highlighting of skills.** I've mentioned how my background has offered me the ability to learn about a major required skill set. For a job that's potentially less relevant (implementing desktop software), I've highlighted how that actually is relevant to the position.
- **Enthusiasm.** I've explained why I'm interested in the position. I don't need to go into a lengthy explanation—a brief mention will do.

If you're sending multiple thank you notes to the same company, you should vary the format and word choice a bit. People talk.

Following Up with Your Recruiter

Although recruiters should be proactive in updating you about your status, they deal with many candidates and sometimes people fall through the cracks. If you haven't heard from your recruiter (and haven't been given a timeline), feel free to e-mail your recruiter after about one week to check in. A simple note like this will suffice:

Hi Jamie,

    I wanted to thank you for helping coordinate my interview last week, and I also wanted to check in about my interview status. Do you know when I could expect an update?

    Thank you!

~Gayle

If there's no response, you can e-mail them after another three working days with a short note like:

> Hi Jamie,
>   I just wanted to check in again. I understand you're probably busy with other work, so I'll probably just give you a call tomorrow or the next day if I haven't heard back from you before then.
>   Thanks!
> ~Gayle

Of course, if at any time your interviewer updates you with a timeline, that timeline completely supersedes this schedule. That is, if your interviewer says you'll hear back in two weeks, you must wait those two weeks, as painful as it is.

Finally, remember the following: companies will always tell you if you're rejected. Always (or at least I've never heard of a company that doesn't). If your recruiter doesn't respond, there can be many reasons for it—but being rejected is not one of them.

Contacting Your References

Before providing the contact information for your references, make sure to check with your references. Confirm with them again that they can be a reference, and use this opportunity to tell them a bit about the position and what skills you'd like them to highlight. References hate to be caught off guard.

Dealing with Rejection

For each offer a company gives out, a company rejects an average of 5 to 10 candidates. That means that, as a candidate, you can expect to get rejected—a lot. It may mean that the position was a poor match, it may mean that you didn't prepare adequately, or it may mean that you just had bad luck.

In the unfortunate case that a company does not extend you an offer, the important thing at this point is to not burn bridges. Companies will usually let you reapply within six months to a year, and a positive relationship with your recruiter is critical for doing this. Try to offer a polite response like, "OK, well I'm sorry to hear that, but thank you very much for the opportunity. I really enjoyed the experience, and I hope to be able to revisit it down the road."

You can also try asking for feedback. It's unlikely that they'll give you feedback, but you will increase your chances if you focus your question in a positive way. That is, the question "Do you have any suggestions as to what I should focus on in my future preparation?" is more likely to get a response than "What did I do poorly?"

Your Questions Answered

Run for the Hills

Dear Gayle,

I've been shy and nervous talking to new people my entire life. I've never liked interviewing, as a result, but I'm really dreading this upcoming interview.

HR has informed me that at the end of the day, I'll be expected to give a short, five-minute talk about a prior project I've done. All the interviewers from that day will be attending, and will have a chance to talk afterwards.

I'm terrified. Any tips?

~L. R.

Dear L. R.,

Run? Just joking.

First, pick a recent project. You'll feel more comfortable with the topic and will get less nervous. You can even dumb down some of the details—they won't know the difference.

Second, tell a story. Introduce the issue you were faced with, and walk them through how you solve it. You probably won't have access to PowerPoint, so use hand gestures to show when you transition from one point to the next.

Third, brainstorm the questions the interviewer is likely to ask, and prepare your answers. They could take the questions two directions: (1) interview-y questions (hardest challenges, etc.), or (2) real-world questions (impact, issues, etc.).

Fourth, practice! In front of a mirror, your friends, or just the family pet.

Finally, admit to your interviewers that you're nervous. They'll probably smile and do what they can to calm you down, and you'll get away from this uber-serious-professional tone.

On a more serious level, though, if you *really* dread public speaking, you may want to reconsider this position. Public speaking is obviously an important enough part of the job that they're putting it into the interview process. Are you prepared to take on a job if this is an integral part?

~Gayle

Too Much Information or Just Enough?

Dear Gayle,

I have Tourette's syndrome. While I don't curse or do any-thing inappropriate (thank God), I do twitch, especially when nervous. Should I give my recruiters a heads-up about this? I'm worried that this may make them uncomfortable or, even worse, open me up to discrimination.

~T. B.

Dear T. B.,

You'll hear advice both ways on this, but I think it really depends on how severe the condition is. Will it distract signifi-cantly from your interview? Would you feel more comfortable if your interviewer knew why you twitch? If the condition is relatively subtle (i.e., noticeable but not distracting), you may not need to say anything. Here's why:

1. **There are no accommodations for you.** You don't need to ask your interviewer to speak lower, talk louder, write larger, and so on. In short, there's no action they should take, so the information would likely not even leave the ears of your recruiter.

2. **It's obviously medical.** If you had, say, a black eye due to recent surgery, you might want to inform your interviewers of this, lest they thing you decided to rough someone up on your way to the office. In this case, though, there's no other way they can inter-pret a tic. It's clearly a medical issue; who cares if it's Tourette's or something else?

As far as I can see, specifying the condition in advance can only hurt you. Some people might assume that you shout out obscene words at random and (unfairly) be concerned about the impact of your condition.

However, if either of these points were wrong—if you did need accommodation or there is an alternate, worse explanation for your condition—then I would suggest telling your recruiter well in advance.

~Gayle

Playing Hard to Get

Dear Gayle,

I interviewed with a company two weeks ago, and they haven't notified me of a decision. I even tried e-mailing the recruiter—no response. Does this mean I'm rejected?

~S. J.

Dear S. J.,

In one word: no. After you interview with a company, they will always tell you if you're rejected.

Delays can happen for many reasons, good, bad, and neutral:

- They are going to give you an offer, but would like to have all their paperwork together.
- They prefer another candidate, but are waiting for her to make a decision. You are their second choice.
- The team is being "reorg'd" and the current head count is unclear.

(continued)

(continued)

- Your recruiter went on vacation.
- The recruiting team is being reorg'd.
- You have a bad/lazy recruiter.
- One of the many people you interviewed with is slow about entering feedback.

You should continue to check in with your recruiter regularly for updates, but no more than once every few days.

~Gayle

Additional Resources

Please visit www.careercup.com for additional preparation resources, and the preparation grid template.

Chapter 8

Interview Questions

"You know how I interview electrical contractors?" Colin Jaques of Canzam Electric said to me over margaritas one day. "I give them a pipe and I tell them to bend it." Suddenly I pictured a Hulk Hogan–type man heaving as he bends a pipe with his bare hands. *He can't be serious?*

"No, no. It's not about strength." Colin reassured me. "It's about how they answer. Do they ask where you want it bent and at what angle, or do they just bend it? You see, we can't have contractors running around bending things at random with no idea what you—or the client—wants." He had a point.

Like this interview question, many interview questions are not what they seem. Too many candidates stress getting the right answer, as though there's always one, single correct answer (in which case, we'd just give candidates tests—think of the time we'd save!). Rather, interview questions are about the process one takes. Do you check your assumptions? Do you think through all possible cases? How do you break down the problem?

General Advice

Erin, a recruiting coordinator from Microsoft, reminds us that "whatever you're asked, you're always answering the question, 'Why should we hire you?' It is the thesis of your interview."

As you're answering questions, think about your personal thesis. What do you bring to the table? Is it your creativity? Your versatile skill set? Your communication and social skills? While it's tempting to say "yes!" to all of these, you'll more effectively communicate your value-add by focusing on just a couple of core skills.

Finally, remember to always be honest—and that a lie by omission is still a lie. If you've ever worked with a dishonest coworker, you'd understand why this is such a deal breaker: they'll take credit for your work, deny their own mistakes, and even possibly get the company in legal trouble. It's just not worth the risk. However, candidates who admit potentially detrimental information are often given a "plus" that more than compensates for the information they reveal. It shows you to be honest—a plus in and of itself—but it also lends credibility to all the great things you say about yourself.

Communication

While some advice is topic specific, communication skills are more universal. Your communication style will both directly and indirectly impact your performance, so keep this advice in mind:

- **Don't interrupt.** Listen fully to your interviewer's question. Interruptions can not only be offensive but suggest poor communication skills. You may also not understand the actual question if you only listen to half of it.
- **Clarify ambiguity.** Many candidates feel so pressured to blurt out an answer immediately that they start stumbling through an answer. Pretty soon, they wind up at the interview

equivalent of a dark dead-end alley. Imagine, for example, you're given an interview question like, "We're considering launching a new product in China. How would you evaluate this decision?" Whether the product is software, a service, or some other variant can drastically change the response. You may assume one, whereas your interviewer assumed another. When you get a question, think through anything that's ambiguous and clarify it. Not only will this help you give a better answer, but your interviewer might be intentionally testing whether you clarify ambiguity. This is an important skill, both on the job and in interviews!

- **Talk out loud.** Because interview questions are really about your approach, not getting the right answer, solving questions out loud is very important. Taking a few moments to think silently is fine, but you should verbalize most of your thought process. This has an added benefit of enabling your interviewer to steer you in the right direction periodically, enabling you to arrive at an optimal answer more quickly.

When You Get Something Wrong

Once, I saw the mythical "perfect" candidate. I wasn't even scheduled to interview him. Google had flown me out to do "batch" interviews for their new Moscow office; eight interviewers, four interviews each per day, five days. I was on one of my rare breaks when I got called in for a last-minute interview. His interviewers, who rarely have a chance to complete more than one of their five "stock" questions, had run out of questions. So they rounded up the rest of us and brought us in. Even my toughest question was no match for him. He whizzed through my questions and we ended his interview day two hours early.

That was the first and last time I saw such a candidate. This means that everyone else—all 150 candidates I've interviewed plus the 1,500 interview packets I've reviewed—made mistakes.

So if you make a mistake, relax. Admit the mistake—your interviewer probably noticed it anyway—and don't be too embarrassed about it. You'll just fit in with all of us—everyone who is not a crazy Russian interviewee.

Acing the Standard Questions

While questions can vary wildly across teams, companies, and positions, there are a few questions that you can be reasonably assured to get. Love 'em or hate 'em, you're bound to get a few of these.

Why Do You Want to Work Here?

As our Microsoft recruiting coordinator, Erin, said, the thesis of your interview, and therefore this question, is why the company should hire you. She goes on to say that you should "understand what motivates you and let that shine through—unless it's money."

The key to this question is answering it in a way that boosts your chances. It's all about your motivations and skills. Think about the skill sets for the job or the area you'll be working in. What excites you? Do you love working with people? Are you fascinated by tough algorithm problems? Do you want to make an impact? Try to keep your answers as specific as possible to the company or even the team. You might even consider mixing in some comments about your background and how the company is a great match for that.

This is also a great time to flex all the research you've done about the company.

Here's a great response for an engineering position at Google:

There are two major reasons. First, I'm really interested in the design of large systems. I've taken a lot of courses on distributing systems and explored this for my senior project. I feel Google is the best place to deepen my knowledge in this area. But, second, and perhaps more importantly, I really believe that the most important thing for any job is to make sure that you're learning a lot. Whereas at many companies you really learn only about your own team, at Google, employees seem to be encouraged to transfer teams, to share knowledge across teams, to do tech talks about their team's architecture, etc. I can't think of any place where I'd learn more than at Google.

In providing this response, the candidate has shown himself to be excited about learning, to have done research on the company, and to be knowledgeable about a core skill set.

Why Are You Leaving Your Job?

One of my standard opening questions was, "What brings you here today?" A candidate could answer many ways. They could explain why they were leaving their current job. They could tell me why the new position was exciting to them. Or the more literal candidate could joke and say "a car," as one candidate, in fact, did.

One unfortunate candidate took the opportunity to rant about her current position. Her work was boring and tedious. Her teammates were too negative and critical. Her boss was sexist and wouldn't promote her. She wasn't learning enough. On and on and on. I dutifully noted her reasons and progressed with more technical questions, which she breezed through. When we discussed her interviewing feedback later, we discovered that all her interviewers noted the same negativity.

Perhaps she had an unfortunate position with her team, but her willingness to flaunt such hostility showed a lack of professionalism and suggested a general negative demeanor. We rejected her—she could have been toxic to the culture.

No matter how bad your situation is, stay positive. Focus on what you're excited about doing at this new position:

My current position has been great in certain ways. It's taught me a lot about communication, negotiations, and how to manage many clients at once. However, new client acquisition is so highly prioritized at my company that I don't have the opportunity to develop more lasting relationships with clients. I'm looking for an opportunity where I can do this.

Assuming that the new position matches this requirement, this would be an excellent response.

Why Should We Hire You?

This question can be stated in many alternative or related ways: "What skills do you think you bring?," "What do you see your role here being?," and so on. Your response to this question should focus on a few core (related) skills or attributes that you think you offer. Aim for exactly three; fewer than three seems weak, more than three loses the interviewer's focus. Back up each with a short amount of evidence.

Example: "I understand that one of your company's core issues has been improving the server uptime. I think I could make a large impact on this issue, for three reasons. First, my current position has offered me a deep background in efficient server programming, which would be valuable on this project. Second, I recognize that this problem requires working with several teams simultaneously, and I have been playing this intermediary role in my current position. Third, I've spent my spare time profiling various open source projects for their memory usage, and this experience has exposed me to a variety of tools and techniques for optimization."

Where Do You See Yourself in Five Years?

OK, I know I said to always be honest, but this may be one case where you need to give a little white lie. Even if you don't see yourself at the company for any more than a couple of years, companies want to know that they're making a good investment in you.

Your answer to this question should be a concrete, achievable goal for where you could be (at the same company) in five years, along with a specific path for how you'd get there. If you aim too high, then the interviewer might feel that the company isn't the right fit for you. If you aim too low, then the interviewer might see you as lacking ambition. You need to get it just right:

While I'm flexible to where the best opportunity to learn and grow is, I hope to take on a new set of responsibilities. I believe that I have the work ethic and people skills to advance into being a team manager within five years, and I think that, with the additional refinement in my technical skills that this current position would offer, I would be ideally suited for such advancement.

Be careful, though, to not raise any red flags. If your response is along the lines of, "I've never really liked coding, so I'd like to move up into management as soon as possible," your ambition could hurt you.

What Are Your Strengths?

You're probably great at many things, but you want to pick a set of three skills that are most relevant to the job and provable, while also being unique. "Intelligence," for example, is probably very applicable as well as provable, but it's also so common that it's bland.

A better set of strengths are things like communication skills, energy, creativity, working well under stress, motivating others, and so on. When you state each one of these, try to cite a specific example. For instance:

I think there are three core strengths. First, I have strong communication skills that have been refined through five years of prior teaching experience. Second, I'm a very creative person. Whether it's writing new song lyrics for my band or designing a novel interface, I'm able to find unique solutions to problems. Third, I am passionate about learning. I recently finished up a certificate in psychology at the local university, and I'm starting a new program now in art history. I may never directly apply this education, but I love learning new things.

What Are Your Weaknesses?

Many years ago, someone started a vicious rumor that your weaknesses should be strengths in disguise: "I think one of my biggest weaknesses is that I work too hard. I just don't know when to stop!" No, really, stop.

Weaknesses should be genuine weaknesses, but not so bad that they're damning. My personal (and honest) answer for this question when I am interviewed is the following:

> *I think I have three main weaknesses. First, I sometimes lack an attention to detail. While this is somewhat good in that it enables me to execute quickly, it also means that I can make careless mistakes. I have learned that I need to double or triple check important work before submitting. Second, I am a very quantitative person, and sometimes I can lose sight of the personal aspect of a decision—whom it impacts and why. I've learned the hard way that I need to consider who all the stakeholders are in a decision, and how they'll react. Third, I am too critical of my own ideas and sometimes those of others. I've largely masked this by focusing on offering positive feedback, but I know I have some room to improve my internal reactions.*

No one would claim that my weaknesses are good things, but would they disqualify me from a position? Probably not, though it does depend on the position (a motivational coach is probably out of the question for me!).

In your weaknesses, be sure to minimize them by showing how you're working on improving them, or how you've managed to negate the issues (such as I do by double checking my work). Additionally, make sure you can back up your weaknesses with concrete examples. If you can't, they probably aren't weaknesses.

Behavioral and Résumé Questions

Behavioral questions are not just about *if* you can come up with an example of, say, your leadership, but about what the example says about you. Do you subtly influence people, gaining their support in advance of a decision? Do you try to motivate the people around you? Or are you a person who finds it easy to diffuse tense or stressful situations?

Your response to behavioral questions will suggest not only what you've accomplished but how you've accomplished it.

What They're Looking For

Behavioral interview questions are usually structured in the form of "tell me about a time when you . . ." and may ask for examples from specific roles or projects. Interviewers are looking for four key attributes:

1. **Résumé verification.** It's easy to carefully wordsmith your résumé such that it's not *technically* lying, but it certainly magnifies your accomplishments. This sort of exaggeration is more challenging when unexpected questions are lobbed at you, and you must come up with examples from your experience.

2. **Getting things done.** The best predictor of future performance is past performance, so interviewers want to understand the issues you have faced and how you've tackled them. In this case, the specific issues you're asked about will likely relate to the position. For a management or team lead position, you'll likely be asked about leadership or about working with struggling employees.

3. **Personality and culture fit.** Your responses to behavioral questions reveal something about your personality. It shows whether you're the type of person who takes charge through analysis or through building relationships, or whether you're outspoken or soft spoken. No one personality trait is inherently better than another, but some might be a better fit for the company culture.

4. **Communication.** Can you respond "off the cuff" in a clear and concise way? Is your communication structured, or do you ramble? Do you speak in an interesting and engaging manner?

How to Approach

SAR (Situation, Action, Result) is an effective way to structure responses to behavioral and other questions in a way that clearly explains what the problem was, what you did, and what the result was.

Question: "Tell me about a challenging interaction with a teammate."

- The **Situation** should include a brief description of the problem. Provide enough details so that the reader can understand what the problem was, but don't offer much more. *On my last project, I was asked to oversee the work of a man who was much older than me. He was working too independently from the rest of my team and not keeping us informed, and this ended up introducing a lot of conflicting work. When I went to discuss the issues with him, he blew up at me—screaming that he had been working since before I was even born.*

- The **Action** describes what you did. It's generally the most important part of the story. *I left the room to let him calm down, and talked to another teammate. She told me that he was actually just very insecure. When I came back the next day, I approached it from the perspective of his helping me. I asked him to help me with understanding his approach, saying that I needed it for some work I was doing. I then checked in on him regularly, explaining that I was confused about how to design some of my work and asked to see what he was doing. This enabled me to refocus some of his work, by asking some questions about how he would deal with specific problems.*

- The **Result** explains what happened, and sometimes what you learned from it.

  Because I never told him he was doing things wrong, he never felt attacked. I merely asked questions and told him when I was confused. With this approach, I was able to stay informed about what he was doing, and gently guide him in the right direction. He was no longer a drain on our team's productivity.

Note how I skipped over a lot of details; I never explained what the project was or what the conflicting work was. It's not relevant to this story.

Five Example Questions

1. Tell me about a time when you gave a presentation to a group of people who disagreed with you.
2. Tell me about the biggest mistake you made on your past project.
3. Tell me about a time when you had to deal with a teammate who was underperforming.
4. Tell me about a time when you had to make a controversial decision.
5. Tell me about a time when you had to use emotional intelligence to lead.

See Appendix B for potential answers to these five questions.

Estimation Questions

How many ping-pong balls would fit in a 747 aircraft? How many pizzas are consumed every year in the United States? I don't know either, but if I did, it wouldn't help me at all on these questions.

These seemingly bizarre questions are not about knowing the right answer, but rather about the process one takes to get there. The relevance of this to real life is debatable, but supporters of these questions argue that being able to ballpark and deduce numbers is valuable.

What They're Looking For

Estimation questions are designed to test your skills in a few areas:

- **Mathematics.** Can you do math in your head? If numbers are too big too easily estimate $(3{,}124 \times 8{,}923)$ can you make a reasonable approximation $(3{,}000 \times 9{,}000 = 27{,}000{,}000)$?
- **Assumptions.** Can you make reasonable assumptions, such as the width of an aircraft? And if you do, (such as the width of an aircraft seat), do you verbally call them out so that people can check them?
- **Deduction/Intelligence.** Can you logically reason through an answer using the facts that you do know?
- **Carefulness.** Do you understand when *not* to generalize? For example, if computing the average amount of money spent on clothing the United States, do you treat adults and children differently?
- **Intuition.** Do you have a good gut feel for when something doesn't sound right? For example, suppose logic leads you to conclude that one million pizzas are delivered each year in the United States—do you understand that that sounds low (one pizza per 300 people per year)?

How to Approach Them

These questions require logically deducing an answer from what you know, and there are often multiple paths to arrive at an answer.

Imagine you are trying to compute how many interviews are conducted each year for programming jobs, for students alone. You can deduce this by calculating how many students graduate from college each year, what percentage are computer science majors, and how many interviews they each do. Explain this thought process to your interviewer before beginning:

- **Number of college graduates.** There are 300 million people in the United States, and the average life span is 75 years. If you assume people are roughly evenly distributed across each year, then 4 million people would be 22 years old. Assume that 25 percent of the United States population graduates college, so that makes one million college graduates each year.
- **Number of computer science majors.** Now, what percent of college graduates have engineering degrees? Based on my own high school and those of my friends, let's assume that 75 percent go to universities (instead of liberal arts colleges). This might be an inaccurate assumption, but we'll go with it. Of those, 20 percent of each university is in the engineering school, and 20 percent of those students are in computer science: 1 million × 75 percent × 20 percent × 20 percent = 30,000 computer science degrees awarded each year.
- **Number of interviews.** Of those, let's say 50 percent go on to take programming jobs, and they interview for an average of five companies, with four interviews per company: 30,000 × 50 percent × 5 × 4 = 300,000. So, we estimate that computer science students do a total of 300,000 interviews per year.

The exact answer might be wrong, but it's not the answer that counts—it's the approach.

Five Example Questions

1. How many golf balls would fit in a school bus?
2. How many pizzas are delivered in New York?
3. How much revenue does the pet food industry make each year?

4. How much would you charge to wash all the streets in New York City?

5. How many people work at fast-food restaurants in the entire world?

Design Questions

Design questions range from the normal ("How would you design a To Do list manager?") to the abnormal ("How would you design an alarm clock for the deaf?"), and are common for many positions, especially program/product managers. They often focus on specific markets: children, deaf people, blind people, and so on.

What They're Looking For

"We want to know if you are customer focused," Joon, a program manager at Microsoft, says. "So 50 percent of this question is being able to put yourself in the shoes of a customer—being able to understand who the target user is. Twenty-five percent is about creativity. Can you come up with a new fresh perspective about how it might work? The remaining 25 percent is communication."

Most candidates focus too much on the creativity aspects—coming up with crazy new features and widgets. While that can be great, is that really what you would do in the real world? Remember that interviewing is supposed to mirror your real-world performance, and in the real world, you'd figure out what the customers want and design for that.

As you answer these questions, remember that interviewers are trying to answer these three questions about you:

- **Are you creative?** Can you think of out of the box to find a novel solution to a problem, or do you pump out small tweaks on the same old stuff?
- **Are you customer focused?** Do you think about what the customer's needs are, or their limitations? A 16-year-old girl

has a lot in common with her parents, but she also has her own unique needs.

- **How do you deal with ambiguity?** Do you recognize elements as being ambiguous, and clarify them? If you can't resolve ambiguity, how do you make a decision?
- **Can you communicate your ideas?** On these questions, it's easy to wind up rambling about an endless set of features. An effective communicator will instead approach this in a structured way, wrapping up at the end with her conclusions.

How to Approach Them

Just for fun, let's take the actual problem I was asked during my Microsoft interview: "Design a key fob for a 16-year-old girl." (*Note:* A key fob is a key/remote for a car.)

Step 1: Resolve Ambiguity

Who is buying the car—the girl or the parents? Is this for a new car or an additional key fob for an existing car? Is it a regular car or an SUV?

The first question is important because it determines who the customer is: just the girl, or the girl and the parents. The second question is important because it determines what the "first-time user" setup is: will it just work, or will it take programming? The third question determines whether or not the key fab needs a button to pop the trunk.

Step 2: What Are the Basic Product Needs?

A key fob must, at the minimum, be able to unlock the car, lock the car, activate the alarm, and pop the trunk.

Step 3: What Does the Customer Need? (And Who Is the Customer?)

A discussion to have with your interviewer is: who drives the purchasing decision for this key fob? Let's assume that the parents are driving the decision, but the girl often offers input.

What do the parents need or care about? Price and safety are probably two of the biggest.

What does the girl care about? Appearance—she wants it to look good. Durability—she's probably throwing it in her purse or backpack.

What else might the girl or the parents care about?

Step 4: What Features Will Meet These Needs?

Appearance: Offer the item in multiple colors with a glossy exterior, and have the key fold out from the key fob.

Durability: We want a durable material, like a hard plastic, that doesn't scratch easily.

Safety: Can we implement a "911" button on the key fab? What about a global positioning system (GPS) tracker—or is this too scary?

One other area to dig deeper into is the purchase process. Can someone "upgrade" to this type of key fab? To what extent should we optimize for this scenario?

Five Example Questions

1. Design a TV remote for six-year-olds.
2. Design an ATM for the blind.
3. If you had an infinite amount of money, how would you design a bathroom?
4. Most people hate bank web sites. Design a web site for a new bank.
5. Design the heating/air-conditioning controls for a car. Assume that you're designing from scratch: no one has ever seen a car's air-conditioning/heating controls.

Brainteasers: Why Are Manhole Covers Round?

Once standard at Microsoft and many other companies, brainteasers have dropped in popularity substantially. Interviewers are instead encouraged to ask behavioral or skill-specific interview questions. Unfortunately, they still pop up from time to time, either because no one can decide exactly what a brainteaser is, or because some interviewers still feel that these questions are an effective way of measuring intelligence.

Luckily, software engineers need not fear these questions: the vast majority of candidates will not face a single brainteaser. Those engineers who do will likely find that the question has a quantitative or computer science basis.

What They're Looking For

Interviewers who ask brainteasers feel (mistakenly, in my opinion) that these questions are an effective measure of intelligence. They want to know if you can tackle a hard problem and logically work toward the answer.

Fortunately, this means that the brainteasers are unlikely to be of the "word trick" variety and more likely to be one that can be approached through logic and deduction.

How to Approach Them

Brainteasers have a wide range, so it's difficult to offer a nice and simple path to tackling them. However, there are a few approaches that I have found work well. One or more of these might be useful in a brainteaser question:

Solve a subproblem

If you find that there is a variation or a subproblem you can solve, you might very well be on the right track. Work with this for a bit and see where you can go.

- **Example:** You have two ropes that burn for exactly one hour each. The ropes are of uneven densities, so half the rope lengthwise might take more than 30 minutes. Use the ropes to time something that is exactly 15 minutes.

- Subproblem: You may realize that you can time 30 minutes by lighting a rope at both ends.
- Solution: Light rope 1 at both ends, and rope 2 at one end. When rope 1 burns up, 30 minutes will have passed and there will be 30 minutes remaining on rope 2. Light rope 2 on the other end and start your timer. Stop your time when rope 2 burns up.

Develop a Rule or Equation

When you get a problem, see if you can work through examples. Try to formulate any rules or equations that you discover along the way as specifically as possible.

- **Example:** You have 100 lockers. Someone starts off by opening every locker. Then they close every second locker. Then they open every fourth, etc. At the end of 100 operations, which lockers will be open?
- Rule #1: The xth locker is toggled on the yth operation if x is divisible by y.
- Rule #2: The xth locker is open at the end of 100 operations if it has an odd number of factors.
- Solution: If you play with some examples, you'll find that almost all numbers have an even number of factors. This is because if a number n is divisible by x, it's also divisible by n/x (sort of like the complement). For example, since 12 is divisible by 3, it must also be divisible by 12/3 (or 4). Thus, the list of factors that a number has can almost always be "paired off." Factors (35) = {1 and 12, 2 and 6, 3 and 4}. The only way that you could wind up with an odd number of factors is if a number is a perfect square: Factors (36) = {1 and 36, 2 and 18, 3 and 12, 4 and 9, 6 and 6}. Therefore, the number of open lockers equals the number of perfect squares. There are 10 perfect squares less than 100: 1^1, 2^2, . . . , 10^{10}.

Simplify the problem

Sometimes simplifying a problem or solving the problem for a specific case can help illustrate a general trend.

- **Example:** A bunch of people are on an island and, one night, some are given magical hats. These hats are magical because they can't see their own hat, but they can see everyone else's. To remove a hat, one must take a swim at exactly midnight (and there are severe penalties to taking a hatless swim). How long does it take the people to remove the hats? *Note:* They know that at least one person has a hat, but they don't know how many.

- Simplification: *What if only one person had a hat?* In this case, the hat wearer would see no one else with a hat, and know it must be him. He would go for a midnight swim. *What two people (let's call them A and B) had hats?* A and B know that there could be either one or two hats out there, but don't know which. They know, however, if there's only one hat, it'll be removed at midnight. When day 2 comes, they must conclude that there are two hats. They know they have the second one, and they both take a swim at midnight. *What if three people have hats?* A, B, and C recognize that there are two possibilities: two hats and three hats. When two nights pass and everyone still has a hat, they all know that there are three hats and they all go for a swim.

- Solution: Extending this out, we can see that if there are c hats, it takes c nights for them all to be removed. All hats are removed simultaneously. From the very first day, each person knows that there are only two possibilities: c hats and $(c - 1)$ hats. If there were $(c - 1)$ hats, they would be removed on the $(c - 1)$th night. The hats are not removed, and so all the hat wearers conclude that there are cth hats on the night.

Examples

- You have 10 bottles of pills. Nine bottles are filled with pills of 1.0 grams, but one has pills of 1.1 grams. With only one use of a scale, how would you figure out which bottle has the heavier pills? *Note:* The scale gives an exact measurement.
- Five coworkers decide that they'd like to compute their average salary. How can they do this without telling anyone their salary?
- There is a building of 100 floors. If an egg drops from the nth floor or above it will break. If it's dropped from any floor below, it will not break. You're given two eggs. Would you find n while minimizing the total number of drops?
- You have a three-gallon jug and a five-gallon jug and an unlimited supply of water. How do you use these to get exactly four gallons of water?
- There is an 8×8 chess board in which two diagonally opposite corners have been cut off. You are given 31 dominoes, and a single domino can cover exactly two squares. Can you use the 31 dominos to cover the entire board?

Answering the Tough Questions

Sometimes, the toughest questions are the ones we already know and don't want to answer. Maybe it's a layoff, maybe it's a pattern of job hopping, or maybe it's a sudden career switch. No matter how much we don't want to get these questions, we must be prepared for them. Practice your story for this, both to yourself out loud and to your friends. Does it appear honest and credible? Are you prepared for any follow-up questions that your interviewer might ask?

The biggest mistake you can make in this question is brushing off the question. Your interviewer may not press you for your answer, but she won't be impressed.

Whatever you're trying to hide, be honest and don't assign too much blame away. Admit your mistake, and focus on what you've learned and how you've grown since then. This sort of answer will show maturity and honesty, while leaving your response on an honest note.

Layoffs

If you were let go during a round of layoffs, you're in a better position than many. However, even these routine layoffs might raise a red flag: some people are usually kept—why weren't you?

The important thing is to stress evidence that you were performing well:

- "The recession hit my company really hard. I was able to survive three rounds of layoffs, but the fourth one included me, too. Frankly, I can't really blame my company: my role is about client service, and there weren't many clients left."
- "My firm laid off about 25 percent of its workforce, and it hit the mobile division the hardest. My manager fought hard for me, but given the new direction of the company, it just didn't make sense."

Being Fired

Interviewers know that there are two sides of the story. If you claim it's not your fault that you got fired, they'll just dig elsewhere and discover the truth eventually. It's better if it comes from you.

Accept the blame, and show what you've learned from it:

- "My company had expectations of working upwards of 70 hours per week. I had a new baby at home, and I couldn't do more than 40 or 50 hours. I held on longer than I should have, but it taught me a valuable lesson about setting mutual expectations up front."

- "I was fired because I was no longer very productive. The truth was that I wasn't excited about the job, which made me lose focus at work. The bright side is that it caused me to shift my career toward my true passion—technology—and I'm really excited about the new direction for my career."

Offer a crisp and concise answer. Don't play the blame game. Don't bad-mouth your former employer. And don't lie.

Unemployment

If you've been unemployed for an extended period of time, interviewers may want to know what you have done during your time off. "Looking for a job" is probably not a complete answer. How many hours a day could you have really spent doing that?

The best answer involves accomplishing something or brushing up on new skills. I recall one man I interviewed who had a seven-year gap (!) in his career. He explained to me that he had taken time off to raise his two young children. Once they started preschool, he spent his day writing a few games and small pieces of software. This candidate spun what was initially a red flag—an extended career gap—into a big plus. Many of us write software for pay, but writing software for fun shows a unique passion for the field. He was hired.

If you're currently unemployed, find something to do that's productive. Can you help out your friend's start-up? Can you take some classes at a community college? Unemployment is an excellent time to beef up your résumé.

Your Questions Answered

Barrier to Entry

Dear Gayle,

I've lived most of my life in India, before relocating to the United States, and still have a very thick accent. This isn't as much of an issue for technical questions, but I have trouble maintaining a conversation with my interviewer on behavioral questions.

If my interviewer is from a country other than India or the United States, this issue is exacerbated. Is there any way to request specific nationalities of interviewers?

~G. E.

Dear G. E.,

You can't ask for specific nationalities and, even if you could, what would that say about you? No one wants to hire someone who can work only with specific nationalities.

Instead, I'd work on how you communicate. Speaking more slowly and using simpler words can help with comprehension.

In the long run, however, you might want to think about speech classes. Many people have reported a lot of success with improving their pronunciation in this way. This would not only help your job search, it would also help your career.

~Gayle

It's a Numbers Game

Dear Gayle,

While I understand the basic approach of estimation questions, I always seem to make mathematical mistakes. I'm just not good at math in my head. Can I ask for a calculator, or is there anything else I can do?

~W. P.

Dear W. P,

You probably can't ask for a calculator, but there are ways that you can get better at these questions, especially since you say you have the approach down.

Many people face difficulty with doing math in their head because they just can't hold so many different numbers at once. As soon as the number 293 comes up, the number 143 gets lost. It may be helpful to ask for a sheet of paper to jot down numbers as you go.

Another trick that may help you is to keep your notes well structured. You might be periodically pulling from the wrong number on the page, causing you to wind up with a wildly inaccurate number.

Finally, memorizing common arithmetic "equations" can be useful. You hopefully have the multiplication tables up through 12-times-12 memorized, but you should memorize up through 20-times-20. Make sure you really, really know them—it's an easy way to improve your results.

~Gayle

The Great Unknown

Dear Gayle,

In a recent interview, I was asked to design a social network for the elderly. I've never used Facebook or any other service, so I didn't know how to answer this question. I explained this to my interviewer, but she just shrugged and asked me to do it anyway.

Isn't this sort of unfair? How was I supposed to handle this question?

~C. R.

Dear C. R.,

In this situation, it was probably a good idea to explain to your interviewer that you had never used a social networking web site. This way she would understand if you made an unusual assumption. However, at that point, your interviewer made the determination that she wanted to hear your answer anyway. She will take into account your situation as necessary.

Your lack of familiarity could either help you or hurt you—it depends on how you take it. If you stomp your foot or act unhappy, well that will really hurt you. After all, in life, sometimes we get asked to design an application we're not familiar with.

In those cases, how do we proceed? We figure out what the needs are. And here's where the potential advantage comes in.

Because you're not familiar with Facebook, you won't be thinking about events or status feeds or "like" buttons—items that were designed with a different user in mind. You'll be

(continued)

(continued)

> solely focused on what elderly people care about: their grand-
> children, their health, and maybe some TV shows and news.
> This means you'll want to make it easy for people to send
> pictures to them. Maybe they'll want to connect with their
> doctors, too. Catch recaps of TV shows. Read short news
> summaries.
>
> When in doubt, most interview questions can be answered
> by pretending it's a real-life situation. In the end, that's what
> interviews are designed to simulate.
> ~Gayle

Additional Resources

Please visit www.careercup.com for additional interview questions
and resources.

Chapter 9

The Programming Interview

If you're applying for a software development position, you've got a special set of skills to prepare. Yes, you'll be asked to code. No, you don't get a computer—just a whiteboard, or sometimes just a sheet of paper. Whiteboard and interviewing coding requires a special set of skills. Even the best coders can get nailed on coding questions.

A software development interview consists of about 15 minutes of discussion, which usually includes some questions about your résumé and/or offers you a chance to ask the interviewer questions. The bulk of the interview is spent on coding and algorithm questions.

Coding questions can be very quick, but will often take up the full interview time. You're not expected to be a flawless coder. Most questions are tricky enough that even the best candidates make a few mistakes.

How They Differ: Microsoft, Google, Amazon, and Apple

I can't tell you what each company will ask—after all, each interviewer basically does whatever he or she wants. However, certain companies have trends.

- **Google** tends to emphasize questions on scalability more than other companies (for instance, "Design a web crawler"). Questions on bit manipulation are also quite common.
- **Amazon** loves object-oriented design questions—I mean really *loves*, in a high-school-crush-you-just-can't-get-over sort of way. They just can't stop asking them. If you're going to interview at Amazon, make sure you study these problems. And, since Amazon is a web-based company, you'll also want to prepare for scalability questions.
- **Microsoft** is all over the map, which is to be expected since it has a pretty diverse set of projects. Its interviewers tend to ask more questions about C and C++. If you don't list the languages on your résumé, you have nothing to fear. However, if you do list these languages, you'll want to make sure that you're comfortable coding in them. Additionally, Microsoft tends to emphasize testing and design skills more in developers than other companies do, so be prepared for these questions.
- **Apple** wants to know that you're as die-hard an Apple fan as the other people in the cult—I mean, company. Make sure you understand Apple's products, especially those of the team you are interviewing with. What would you improve about the product? Remember that Apple has a lot of smart people who haven't yet done what you're suggesting. Think about why they haven't.

How to Prepare

When it comes to practicing interview questions, quality matters more than quantity. There are literally thousands of sample interview questions online for companies like Google, Microsoft, and Amazon—don't try to memorize the answers. It's impossible and won't help you anyway!

The Five-Step Approach to Effective Preparation

Take your time solving problems, and try the following approach in practicing questions:

1. **Try to solve the problem on your own.** I mean, *really* try to solve it. Many questions are designed to be tough—that's OK! When you're solving a problem, make sure to think about both the space and time complexity. Ask yourself if you could improve the time efficiency by reducing the space efficiency.

2. **Write the code for the algorithm on paper.** You've been coding all your life on a computer, and you've gotten used to the many nice things about it: compilers, code completion, and so on. You won't have any of these in an interview, so you better get used to it now. Implement the code the old-fashioned way, down to every last semicolon.

3. **Test your code!** By hand, that is. No cheating with a computer!

4. **Type your code into a computer exactly as is.** Rerun both the test cases you tried and some new ones.

5. **Start a list of all the mistakes you made, and analyze what types of mistakes you make the most often.** Is it specific mistakes?

You can find thousands of coding interview questions on CareerCup.com that candidates have gotten from companies like Google, Microsoft, Amazon, and other major tech companies.

What If I Hear a Question I Know?

In offering thousands of sample interview questions on CareerCup .com and in my other book, *Cracking the Coding Interview*, my goal is not to help you memorize questions and then regurgitate answers in an interview. Interviewers want to see how you approach problems, so spitting out pre-prepared solutions won't do you much good.

If you get a question you've heard before, tell your interviewer! It's not only the *right* thing to do; it's also the smart thing. If you try to hide it and pretend to fumble through the answer, your interviewer will probably be suspicious—and lying (or hiding the truth) is perhaps the worst thing you could do in an interview.

However, if you are honest and say that you've heard the question before, you'll win major bonus points. Interviewers care about honesty, even if there's usually no way to directly test it.

"Must Know" Topics

Most interviewers won't ask you about specific algorithms for binary tree balancing or other complex algorithms. Frankly, they probably don't remember these algorithms either. (Yes, that means you can put down the CLRS algorithms book.)

You're usually expected to know only the basics. Here's a list of the absolute must-know topics:

This is not, of course, an all-inclusive list. Questions may be asked on areas outside of these topics. This is merely a "must know" list.

Data Structures	Algorithms	Concepts
Linked Lists	Breadth First Search	Bit Manipulation
Binary Trees	Depth First Search	Singleton Design Pattern
Tries	Binary Search	Factory Design Pattern
Stacks	Merge Sort	Memory (Stack vs. Heap)
Queues	Quick Sort	Recursion
Vectors/ArrayLists	Tree Insert/Find/etc.	Big-O Time
Hash Tables		

For each of the topics, make sure you understand how to implement/use them, and (where applicable) the space and time complexity.

Practice implementing the data structures and algorithms. You might be asked to implement them directly, or you might be asked to implement a modification of them. Either way, the more comfortable you are with the implementations, the better.

Memory Usage

As you're reviewing data structures, remember to practice computing the memory usage of a data structure or an algorithm. Your interviewer might directly ask you much memory something takes, or you might need to compute this yourself if your problem involves large amounts of data.

- **Data structures.** Don't forget to include the pointers to other data. For example, a doubly linked list that holds 1,000 integers will often use about 12KB of memory (4 bytes for the data, 4 bytes for the previous pointer, and 4 bytes for the next pointer). This means that making a singly linked list into a doubly linked list can dramatically increase memory usage.

- **Algorithms.** A recursive algorithm often takes up dramatically more space than an iterative algorithm. Consider, for example, an algorithm to compute the jth to last element of a singly linked list. An approach that uses an array to sort each element may be no better than a recursive algorithm—both use O(n) memory! (The best solution involves using two pointers, where one starts off j spaces ahead.)

Many candidates think of their algorithms on only one dimension—time—but it's important to consider the space complexity as well. We must often make a trade-off between time and space, and sometimes, we *do* sacrifice time efficiency to reduce memory usage.

Coding Questions

Interviews are supposed to be difficult. If you don't get every—or any—answer immediately, that's OK! In fact, in my experience, maybe only 10 people out of the 150+ that I've interviewed have gotten the algorithm right instantly, and all but one of them made later mistakes on the coding.

So when you get a hard question, don't panic. Just start talking aloud about how you would solve it.

And, remember: you're not done until the interviewer says that you're done! What I mean here is that when you come up with an algorithm, start thinking about the problems accompanying it. When you write code, start trying to find bugs. If you're anything like the other 110 candidates that I've interviewed, you probably made some mistakes.

1. Ask your interviewer questions to resolve ambiguity.
2. Design an algorithm.

3. Write pseudo-code first, but make sure to tell your interviewer that you're writing pseudo-code! Otherwise, he/she may think that you're never planning to write "real" code, and many interviewers will hold that against you.

4. Write your code, not too slow and not too fast.

5. Test your code and *carefully* fix any mistakes.

Let's go into each of these in more detail.

Step 1: Ask Questions

Technical problems are more ambiguous than they might appear, so make sure to ask questions to resolve anything that might be unclear or ambiguous. You may eventually wind up with a very different—or much easier—problem than you had initially thought. In fact, many interviewers (especially at Microsoft) will specifically test to see if you ask good questions.

Good questions might be things like: What are the data types? How much data is there? What assumptions do you need to solve the problem? Who is the user?

Example: "Design an Algorithm to Sort a List"

- **Question:** What sort of list? An array? A linked list?
  Answer: An array.
- **Question:** What does the array hold? Numbers? Characters? Strings?
  Answer: Numbers.
- **Question:** And are the numbers integers?
  Answer: Yes.
- **Question:** Where did the numbers come from? Are they IDs? Values of something?
  Answer: They are the ages of customers.
- **Question:** And how many customers are there?
  Answer: About a million.

We now have a pretty different problem: sort an array containing a million integers between 0 and 130 (I don't think people are living past age 130, are they?). How do we solve this? Just create an array with 130 elements and count the number of ages at each value.

Step 2: Design an Algorithm

Designing an algorithm can be tough, but our five approaches to algorithms can help you out. While you're designing your algorithm, don't forget to think about:

- What are the space and time complexities?
- What happens if there is a lot of data?
- Does your design cause other issues? (i.e., if you're creating a modified version of a binary search tree, did your design impact the time for insert/find/delete?)
- If there are other issues, did you make the right trade-offs?
- If they gave you specific data (e.g., mentioned that the data is ages, or in sorted order), have you leveraged that information? There's probably a reason that you're given it.

Step 3: Pseudo-Code

Writing pseudo-code first can help you outline your thoughts clearly and reduce the number of mistakes you commit. But make sure to tell your interviewer that you're writing pseudo-code first and that you'll follow it up with "real" code. Many candidates will write pseudo-code in order to "escape" writing real code, and you certainly don't want to be confused with those candidates.

Step 4: Code

You don't need to rush through your code; in fact, this will most likely hurt you. Just go at a nice, slow methodical pace and remember this advice:

- **Use data structures generously.** Where relevant, use a good data structure or define your own. For example, if you're asked a problem involving finding the minimum age for a group of people, consider defining a data structure to represent a Person. This shows your interviewer that you care about good object-oriented design.
- **Don't crowd your code.** Many candidates will start writing their code in the middle of the whiteboard. This is fine for the first few lines. But whiteboards aren't that big. Pretty soon they wind up with arrows all over the board directing the interviewer to the next line of code. We'd never hold it against a candidate, but it's still distracting for everyone.

Step 5: Test

Yes, you need to test your code! Consider testing for:

- Extreme cases: 0, negative, null, maximums, etc.
- User error: What happens if the user passes in null or a negative value?
- General cases: Test the normal case.

If the algorithm is complicated or highly numerical (bit shifting, arithmetic, etc.), consider testing while you're writing the code rather than just at the end.

When you find a mistake (which you will), relax. Almost no one writes bug-free code; what's important is how you react to it. Point out the mistake, and carefully analyze why the bug is occurring. Is it really just when you pass in 0, or does it happen in other cases, too?

I remember one candidate who was implementing a binary search tree method getSize(). When he realized that his method returned "3" on a two-element tree, he quickly appended a "+ 1" to the return statement. Maybe he thought I wouldn't notice. A few moments later, he discovered his algorithm branched left in one case instead of right. So he flipped the left and right. Pretty soon, his code was so littered with little changes that it was unrecognizable; he had to start over from scratch.

This approach, which I've seen far too many times, seems somewhat like throwing Scrabble letters across the room, hoping they'll spell a word when they land. Sure, it *could* happen—but it still wouldn't make you a good speller.

Algorithm Questions: Five Ways to Create an Algorithm

There's no surefire approach to solving a tricky algorithm problem, but the following approaches can be useful. Keep in mind that the more problems you practice, the easier it will be to identify which approach to use.

Also, remember that the five approaches can be "mixed and matched." That is, once you've applied "Simplify and Generalize," you may want to implement Pattern Matching next.

Approach 1: Examplify

We start with Examplify, since it's probably the most well-known (though not by name). Examplify simply means to write out specific examples of the problem and see if you can figure out a general rule.

Example: Given a time, calculate the angle between the hour and minute hands on a clock.

Start with an example like 3:27. We can draw a picture of a clock by selecting where the 3-hour hand is and where the 27-minute hand is. Note that the hour hand moves continuously, not in a discrete jump when the time changes.

By playing around with examples, we can develop a rule:

- Minute angle (from 12 o'clock): 360 × minutes / 60

- Hour angle (from 12 o'clock): 360 $\times$ (hour % 12) / 12 + 360 $\times$ (minutes / 60) $\times$ (1 / 12)
- Angle between hour and minute: (hour angle – minute angle) % 360

By simple arithmetic, this reduces to 30 $\times$ hours – 5.5 $\times$ minutes.

Approach 2: Pattern Matching

Pattern matching means to relate a problem to similar ones, and figure out if you can modify the solution to solve the new problem. This is one reason why practicing lots of problems is important; the more problems you do, the better you get.

Example: A sorted array has been rotated so that the elements might appear in the order 3 4 5 6 7 1 2. How would you find the minimum element?

This question is most similar to the following two well-known problems:

- Find the minimum element in an unsorted array.
- Find a specific element in an array (e.g., binary search).

Finding the minimum element in an unsorted array isn't a particularly interesting algorithm (you could just iterate through all the elements), nor does it use the information provided (that the array is sorted). It's unlikely to be useful here.

However, binary search is very applicable. You know that the array is sorted but rotated. So it must proceed in an increasing order, then reset and increase again. The minimum element is the "reset" point.

If you compare the first and middle elements (3 and 6), you know that the range is still increasing. This means that the reset point must be after the 6 (or 3 is the minimum element and the array was never rotated). We can continue to apply the lessons from binary search to pinpoint this reset point, by looking for ranges where LEFT $>$ RIGHT. That is, for a particular point, if LEFT $<$ RIGHT, then the range does not contain the reset. If LEFT $>$ RIGHT, then it does.

Approach 3: Simplify and Generalize

In Simplify and Generalize, we change constraints (data type, size, etc.) to simplify the problem, and then try to solve the simplified problem. Once you have an algorithm for the "simplified" problem, you can generalize the problem back to its original form. Can you apply the new lessons?

Example: A ransom note can be formed by cutting words out of a magazine to form a new sentence. How would you figure out if a ransom note (string) can be formed from a given magazine (string)?

We can simplify the problem as follows: instead of solving the problem with words, solve it with characters. That is, imagine we are cutting characters out of a magazine to form a ransom note.

We can solve the simplified ransom note problem with characters by simply creating an array and counting the characters. Each spot in the array corresponds to one letter. First, we count the number of times each character in the ransom note appears, and then we go through the magazine to see if we have all of those characters.

When we generalize the algorithm, we do a very similar thing. This time, rather than creating an array with character counts, we create a hash table. Each word maps to the number of times the word appears.

Approach 4: Base Case and Build

Base Case and Build suggests that we solve the algorithm first for a base case (e.g., just one element). Then, try to solve it for elements one and two, assuming that you have the answer for element one. Then, try to solve it for elements one, two, and three, assuming that you have the answer to elements one and two.

You will notice that Base Case and Build algorithms often lead to natural recursive algorithms.

Example: Design an algorithm to print all permutations of a string. For simplicity, assume all characters are unique.

Consider the following string: abcdefg

- Case "a" → {a}
- Case "ab" → {ab, ba}
- Case "abc" → ?

This is the first "interesting" case. If we had the answer to P("ab"), how could we generate P("abc")? Well, the additional letter is "c," so we can just stick c in at every possible point. That is:

- merge(c, ab) → cab, acb, abc
- merge(c, ba) → cba, bca, bac

We can use a recursive algorithm to solve this problem. First, generate all permutations of a string by "chopping off" the last character and generating all permutations of s[1 . . . n-1]. Then, insert s[n] into every location of the string.

Approach 5: Data Structure Brainstorm

The Data Structure Brainstorm approach admittedly feels somewhat hacky, but it often works. In this approach, we simply run through a list of data structures and try to apply each one. This approach works because many algorithms are quite straightforward once we find the right data structure.

Example: Numbers are randomly generated and stored into an (expanding) array. How would you keep track of the median?

Data Structure Brainstorm:

- Linked list? Probably not—linked lists tend not to do very well with accessing and sorting numbers.

- Array? Maybe, but you already have an array. Could you somehow keep the elements sorted? That's probably expensive. Let's hold off on this and return to it if it's needed.

- Binary tree? This is possible, since binary trees do fairly well with ordering. In fact, if the binary search tree is perfectly balanced, the top might be the median. But, be careful—if there's an even number of elements, the median is actually the average of the middle two elements. The middle two elements can't both be at the top. This is probably a workable algorithm, but let's come back to it.

- Heap? A heap is really good at basic ordering and keeping track of max and mins. This is actually interesting—if you had two heaps, you could keep track of the biggest half and the smallest half of the elements. The biggest half is kept in a min heap, such that the smallest element in the biggest half is at the root. The smallest half is kept in a max heap, such that the biggest element of the smallest half is at the root. Now, with these data structures, you have the potential median elements at the roots. If the heaps are no longer the same size, you can quickly "rebalance" the heaps by popping an element off the one heap and pushing it onto the other.

Note that the more problems you do, the more developed your instinct on which data structure to apply will be. Hash tables, trees, tries, and heaps are some of the best data structures to solve problems.

Object-Oriented Design

Object-oriented design (OOD) questions come in two flavors: OOD for a piece of software and OOD for a real-world object. Despite the seemingly huge difference between these topics, they're approached much the same way:

1. **What are your goals?** Imagine, for example, you are asked to design the classes for a generic deck of cards. What kind of cards? Are they standard playing cards, UNO cards, or some other kind? Just how "generic" is it supposed to be?

2. **What are the core objects?** For example, if you're doing the OOD for a restaurant, your core objects might be Restaurant, Patron, Party, Host, Server, Busser, Table, and so on. Each of these will become a class.

3. **How do the objects relate to each other?** There is probably only one Restaurant, so this can be a singleton class. Restaurant has many Servers, one Host, many Bussers, many Tables, many Parties, and many Patrons. (*Note:* This is just an assumption; talk to your interviewer about this). Each Table has one Server and one Party. Look for and remove redundancies. For example, Restaurant may not need a list of Patrons, since it can get that from the list of Parties.

4. **How do the objects interact?** Think about what the major actions that occur in the restaurant are. For example, a Party makes a Reservation with a Host. The Host sits the Party at a Table and assigns them a Server. Each of these actions should generally correspond to one or more methods. By walking through these methods, you may discover that you missed some objects or that your design isn't quite right. That's OK—now is a great time to add them!

5. **Are there any tricky algorithms?** In some cases, there may be an algorithm that impacts the design. For example, implementing findNextReservation(int partySize) might require some changes to how the reservations are referenced. Discuss these details with your interviewer.

Remember that object-oriented design questions require a lot of communication with your interviewer about how flexible your design should be and how to balance certain trade-offs. There is no "right" answer to an object-oriented design question.

Scalability Questions

When I interviewed at Google, I didn't know a thing about large systems. Sure, I'd taken a distributed computing course where we studied election algorithms and whatnot, but that had nothing to do with what I was asked. Sort a million numbers? Design a web crawler? Yikes!

I fumbled my way through the problem, and I realized I could do this just fine. Once I forgot that I had no idea what I was doing, I learned that I actually understood the primary complexities of large amounts of data and dealing with multiple systems at once.

All I needed to do was take things step by step. Imagine, for instance, that we're designing a hypothetical system X for millions of items (users, files, etc.):

1. How would you solve the problem for a small number of items? Develop an algorithm for this case, which is often pretty straightforward.

2. What happens when you try to implement that algorithm with millions of items? It's likely that you have run out of space on the computer. So, divide up the files across many computers.

   - How do you divide up data across many machines? That is, do the first 100 items appear on the same computer? Or all items with the same hash value mod 100?

   - About how many computers will you need? To estimate this, ask how big each item is, and take a guess at (or ask your interviewer) how much space a typical computer has.

3. Now, fix the problems that occur when you are using many computers. Make sure to answer the following questions:
   - How does one machine know which machine it should access to look up data?
   - Can data get out of sync across computers? How do you handle that?
   - How can you minimize expensive reads across computers?

Testing Interviews

Testers have many names: tester, software design engineer in test, software test engineer, quality assurance, and hey-you-over-there-why-doesn't-this-work. These titles can mean slightly different things depending on the company.

Whatever you call them, testers have a raw deal; not only do they have to master the coding questions, but they also must master testing questions. They must practice coding, algorithms, and data structures on top of the all usual testing problems. If you're a tester, do yourself a favor and make sure to practice coding—it's an excellent way to set yourself apart.

True testing questions usually fall into one of three categories:

1. How would you test this real-world object?
2. Explain how you would test this piece of computer software.
3. Test a method (possibly one that you just wrote).

Testing a Real-World Object

What does testing paper clips and pens have to do with testing Office or Gmail? Perhaps not a ton, but your interviewer certainly thinks they do. Your interviewer is using this question to test your ability to deal with ambiguity, to understand your ability to think about the expected and unexpected behavior, and, as always, to test your ability to structure and communicate your thoughts.

Let's work through this recommended approach for an example problem: test a pen.

1. **Ask questions to understand what the object is.** A pen doesn't seem that ambiguous, but it is. A pen could be anything from a fountain pen, to a child's marker with multiple colors, to a pen for astronauts. Ask your interviewer questions to resolve this ambiguity. Find out who the users are, and what the pen is being used for.

2. **Who is using it, and what are they doing with it?** Small children with poor dexterity are drawing with it, so it probably needs to be nice and thick. They'll probably be drawing on paper on the floor, but this means that they might end up drawing on the floor a bit.

3. **What are the unexpected uses?** Eating it—kids will put anything in their mouths. Drawing on other children or the walls (as my mother once discovered at her friend's house when she interrupted my sister playing a fun game called "Can I draw a solid line through the entire upstairs?"). Stomping on it. Throwing it.

4. **Are there additional stress cases?** Think about hot weather, cold weather, and so on. Not all of these will be applicable in every problem.

5. **Can you fail gracefully?** Ideally, we want our pen to never break. But if it does, can we prevent it from exploding?

6. **What are the test cases?** At this point, we've discovered that we probably want to test for at least the following elements:

   a. Nontoxic. Perhaps we discuss the ingredients with poison control, which might be able to offer more specific tests if necessary.

   b. Washable. Test drawing on floors, walls, clothing, and skin.

   c. Thickness. We'll probably want to conduct a series of tests to understand what widths are uncomfortable for children, in addition to "live testing" our prototype pen.

   d. Softness/Lightness. The material should be a lightweight plastic, so that it doesn't hurt too much it if hits you.

   e. Durability. The pen should not break easily. We should discuss with our interviewer precise measurements about how much pressure it needs to withstand.

   f. Leakage. If the pen does break, we want to make sure that the ink doesn't explode.

You may notice how testing fits into design—this is to be expected. After all, testers need to analyze whether the object fits the design requirements.

Testing a Piece of Software

Now that we've gotten what many consider to be the hardest questions out of the way, testing a piece of software isn't terribly hard. In fact, you approach it much the same way as a "real-world object" question.

Example: Explain how you would test an e-mail client.

1. **Ask questions to resolve ambiguity.** Not all e-mail clients are the same. Is it a corporate e-mail client? A personal e-mail client? Is it a web-based e-mail client, or desktop?

2. **Who is the user?** A corporate user will have very different needs than a personal user, in terms of security, storage, maintenance, and so on.

3. **What is the feature set?** Some features you can probably assume (check e-mail, send e-mail, etc.), but other features may take more of a conversation. Does the e-mail sit on a server? Is it encrypted?

4. **Are there unexpected uses or stress cases?** In the case of an e-mail client, this might mean a flood of e-mail, huge attachments, and the like.

5. **When there are failures, what can you do to fail gracefully?** If a file is too large to be handled by the e-mail client, you will want to make sure that it fails gracefully. That is, the client should at most reject the attachment, but should not permanently freeze.

6. **What can be automated, and what must be manually tested?** Of course, there is an almost endless set of things that you can test—after all, they have full teams to do this. What's important is that you focus on the biggest (or most interesting) items and discuss how you might test it. What can be automated, and what must be manually tested?

Test a Method

After writing code, you might be asked to test the code or perhaps just to generate the test cases. In your test cases, remember to consider the following:

Example: Test a method that sorts an array.

1. **As always, ask questions to resolve ambiguity.** Should the array be sorted in ascending or descending order? What are the expectations as far as time, memory usage, and the like? What data type is the array supposed to have?

2. **What do you need to test for?** Make a list of everything that needs to be checked. In many cases, this might be just the result (e.g., is the array sorted?), but in other cases you might want to check for additional side effects (e.g., memory usage, other data being changed, etc.).

3. **Write the expected cases.** This is the easy one: one of your test cases should simply be an unsorted array.

4. Write the extreme cases. Check for null, empty arrays; huge arrays; already sorted arrays; and so on.

Example Problems

1. Design an algorithm to figure out if someone has won in a game of tic-tac-toe.

2. Given an image represented by an NxN matrix, where each pixel in the image is 4 bytes, write a method to rotate the image by 90 degrees. Can you do this in place?

3. You have two numbers represented by a linked list, where each node contains a single digit. The digits are stored in reverse order, such that the 1's digit is at the head of the list. Write a function that adds the two numbers and returns the sum as a linked list.

    ```
    Input: (3 -> 1 -> 5) 1 (5 -> 9 -> 2)
    Output: 8 -> 0 -> 8
    ```

4. You are given an array of integers (both positive and negative). Find the continuous sequence with the largest sum. Return only the sum.

    ```
    Input: {2, -8, 3, -2, 4, -10}
    Output: 5. (i.e., {3, 2, 4}).
    ```

5. Implement a MyQueue class, which implements a queue using two stacks.

6. Write an algorithm to find the "next" node (i.e., in-order successor) of a given node in a binary search tree where each node has a link to its parent.

7. Design the OOD for a deck of cards. Explain how you would implement a Shuffle() method.

8. Describe an algorithm to find the largest one million numbers in one billion numbers. Assume that the computer memory can hold all one billion numbers.

9. Given two words of equal length that are in a dictionary, write a method to transform one word into another word

by changing only one letter at a time. The new word you get in each step must be in the dictionary.

Input: DAMP, LIKE

Output: DAMP -> LAMP -> LIME -> LIKE

10. Given an NxN matrix of positive and negative integers, write code to find the submatrix with the largest possible sum.

Your Questions Answered

Too Much Prep, Too Little Time

Dear Gayle,

I've been working for a few years as a software programmer at a consulting company, but my work is boring and mostly code maintenance. The little code I write is in C—there is no object-oriented programming. I don't feel like I'm learning much, and I'm definitely not moving up.

My dream is to work for a big company like Microsoft. I feel that I would need months to prepare for these interviews. Should I quit now so that I can focus on preparing?

~R. H.

Dear R. H.,

I'll be honest—I'm not crazy about the idea of quitting just to do interview prep. First, Microsoft and companies like it hire fewer than 5 percent of applicants. Even with a lot of prep, your chances are slim. Second, you'll need to give interviewers an explanation for why you quit, and "to prepare for you" is not a good reason. (It's kind of like telling a woman on the first date that you spent all week preparing for the night. Kind of overkill, don't you think?) Third, the value of intensive, long-term preparation really depends on what your weaknesses are. All you've mentioned is a lack of knowledge about objected-oriented programming, and you probably don't need three months to learn that.

I'd recommend quitting only if you can answer "Yes" to the following questions: (1) you know you can find a job just as good as your current one without any prep; (2) you can't prepare simultaneously with working; (3) it'll take you a long time to prepare.

If you've decided to quit, I'd recommend doing something a bit more tangible with your time. Rather than focusing just on acing the interview, spend your time creating what could be a company. Build a piece of software or a web site, and use this as your primary tool to learn what you need to know (object-oriented programming, etc.).

The benefit of this is that when employers ask you what you've been doing since you quit, you can tell them that you wanted to try to start a company, but you realized it wasn't for you (you discovered that you prefer working with larger teams, etc.). And you'll have something tangible to list on your résumé that'll show experience and mask any gaps.

~Gayle

Know It All

Dear Gayle,

In preparation for my Google interview, I've gone through the coursework for all my prior computer science courses. I've spent the most time on algorithms, and specifically dynamic programming and tree balancing. I'm still not sure I'll be able to complete a problem like this during an interview. Complex algorithm + lots of code = too much time.

How do successful candidates tackle these questions?
~K. T.

Dear K. T.,

Let's take a step and put ourselves in the mind of our interviewers. They want to know if we're smart and if we can code. Having specific knowledge is not important, unless it's either (1) necessary for performing well on the job, or (2) so integral to a basic CS education that no respectable programmer could not know this information and still call themselves an engineer. Inserting an element in a tree falls into category 2. Trees are not actually used that often in industry, but they're so fundamental, how could you *not* know them?

Tree balancing, however, does not. You should know that tree balancing exists, and you should know basically how it works (rotations when the sides get too uneven), but the little details are not that essential to know. Skip it.

Dynamic programming is usually just too complex for an interview. It does get asked, but it's rare, and probably not a good use of your time for preparation. Besides, there isn't that much to the concept. You just need to know that sometimes you can optimize an algorithm by caching the results.

Remember, also, that code in an interview is relatively short. You usually don't write more than 20 lines. Between designing an algorithm, testing the code, and fixing mistakes, there just isn't enough time to write much more than that.

So relax. Focus on preparing for normal range questions— the kinds that you can tackle in 45 minutes.

~Gayle

Misleading Information

Dear Gayle,

I interviewed with Microsoft and I was asked a tough question. I started to think of a brute force solution, and the interviewer said that brute force is fine. I began to write the code, and before I was even finished, the interviewer began to bombard me with questions. His questions then led me to a better solution. I also noticed later that I had some bugs and other mistakes in my code, but these seemed fairly minor.

I feel that he misled me in telling me that my initial solution was fine, and I ended up getting a reject as a result. Do I have any chance to put up an argument?

~D. W.

Dear D. W.,

There's a lot going on in this question, so let me break this down.

1. Did your interviewer mislead you in telling you that brute force is fine (when it really wasn't)?

It is possible you got a bad interviewer who didn't direct you properly. Bad interviewers do exist, even at the best companies. I suspect that your interviewer was probably looking for whether or not you would notice and look for a more optimal solution, or if you would be satisfied with a "good enough" solution. Depending on how far along you were in your interview, the interviewer may also have been thinking, "OK, we don't have much time, and I want to make sure I see this candidate's code. Let me encourage him to just get on with it."

2. Did this cause you to be rejected?

Again, very hard to say that this really caused the reject. First, typically about 75 percent of candidates are rejected at each stage, so it's almost like you have to do things really, really right to not get rejected. Second, it's unlikely to be any one issue that caused a reject. As you noted, you had some bugs and other mistakes. I'd guess that your interviewer's thought was more like, "Hmm, I liked this guy, but his solution wasn't very good, and he had some bugs in his code and a few other mistakes."

3. Can you put up an argument?

No. In high school, did you ever try to argue a case to your principal that a teacher did something wrong? Did they ever side with you? Unless your teacher's actions were egregious, your principal almost certainly sided with your teacher. This is much the same way. Whatever you say to your recruiter, he/she will almost certainly side with your interviewer. You're more likely to spoil your decent reputation at the company, and it's just not worth it.

That said, there are times when you should not stay silent about an interviewer's behavior. If they say anything or do anything offensive, speak up! Or if your recruiter asks for your feedback, then you are welcome to share it.

I'm sorry things didn't work out for you, but you're not alone. Interviews are hard and, unfortunately, very random. Most of my coworkers at Google admitted that they didn't think they'd pass the interviews the second time around. Luckily, most companies understand this and let you apply again in six months to a year.

~Gayle

Additional Resources

Please visit www.careercup.com for thousands of potential interview questions and answers.

Chapter 10

Getting into Gaming

I got off the elevator onto PopCap Games' floor and was instantly hit by memories from my college years. Two engineers, clad in the shorts and jeans apparel that is typical of their role, played a giant version of the classic game Bejeweled. The screen stretched over half the length of their bodies and chimed loudly as they swiped jewels with their full hands. I steered clear. This game single-handedly accounted for my downfall on more than one homework assignment from college, and I refused to get sucked in again.

The super-sized screen, the multicolored walls, entire rooms dedicated to ping-pong—all typical of gaming companies. Even among technology firms, gaming companies stand out for their high-energy environment. They are the new "dot-coms," and venture capitalists everywhere are crossing their fingers and hoping they don't meet the same fate.

The Culture: Is It All Fun and Games?

Alessandra, from gaming recruiting firm VonChurch, suggests that the festive atmosphere is integral to the nature of the field. "Gaming means blending the creative with the techy. Technology firms are already young, fun-filled environments. When you mix in a highly creative workforce, this is what you get."

Her colleague Katy Haddix concurs, but cautions that it's a work hard/play hard atmosphere. "You are expected to be full-seat-in, working 10 to 12 hours per day, plus the weekends when necessary."

Long hours are a necessity in the casual gaming world. Casual games fly from conception to release in a mere two months. Finishing a project before a deadline is always a race, and in this industry, there is always a deadline looming. The work can't stop.

Moreover, your product is live 24 hours per day and often resides on another live and changing platform like Facebook. Things could break at any time; someone needs to be watching it.

In the console gaming world, release cycles are longer, which reduces the stress level, but the hours can still be intense. The entire gaming industry is fiercely competitive.

It is an industry for those truly passionate about games. If you aren't prepared for long hours—complemented, of course, by happy hours and foosball tournaments—then this is not the field for you.

Job Positions: What Can You Do?

Game creation is performed by four core roles: developers, producers, artists, and designers. A handful of other positions, from marketing to quality assurance, assist the game creation, release, and postproduction responsibilities. In this section we will cover what background, skills, and traits you need to have for each of these roles.

Software Engineering

Software engineering hiring at gaming companies is similar to that of other technology companies. "Candidates should expect to be grilled just like they would at Microsoft or any other tech company. We're just like them—we need people who are smart and can code," notes PopCap producer Ben Ahroni.

Because gaming firms move so quickly, they often cannot afford to wait for candidates to get up to speed with their technologies. A candidate who is already well versed in the company's pet language will fare much better in the recruiting process.

Audra Aulabaugh, a recruiter for Big Fish Games, adds that college students interested in gaming enroll in some related courses. "We do hire straight out of college, even without a gaming background, but a proven interest and background in gaming will help set you apart."

Production

Producers fill much of the same role as program managers do in a tech company. They manage the full production of the game, including the prerelease schedule and the postrelease performance. In addition, Ben Ahroni tells me, "the producer must be a leader. When things get tough, you need to be there to raise team morale."

BJ Bigley from Big Kind Games puts it a bit more bluntly. "Producers are socialites. You need to be able to keep everyone happy while getting results. You are the ultimate diplomat."

Being able to write code is nice, but not strictly necessary. What's more important is that you are analytical and quantitative, and that can come from anything from engineering to economics. After the release of the game, the producer must crunch the numbers to understand what's working and what's not. What is the download conversation rate? How many credits do people purchase for each increase in level, and how does this affect their lifetime usage rate?

Producers are most commonly recruited from these two positions:

- **Quality assurance (QA)/testing.** Many producers start off in QA, and specifically in so-called "smoke testing." These roles enable them to see the full gaming life cycle, which translates nicely to the production role. Producers may also come from automation testing, or even from core software development, but this tends to be rarer for the simple reason that coders tend to like to stay coders.

- **Consulting.** Former consultants, particularly from top firms like McKinsey, Bain, and BCG, can make excellent producers. They may lack the gaming industry background, but they have acquired in their prior jobs another useful set of skills. Their jobs developed their analytical approach to problem solving, while also requiring them to interface with a diversity of people and react quickly to issues.

If your résumé lacks both of these positions but you dream of being a producer, don't fret. "Other metric- and data-driven roles, such as online advertising, can also be a natural fit," says Alessandra from VonChurch.

Art

Artists tend to come from traditional art backgrounds, sometimes directly hired from art institutes. Candidates should expect to supply a portfolio and are strongly encouraged to have this posted on their web site.

Hiring can be extremely subjective. It's not always about who draws the best, but rather who draws the best for the team. Understanding what style of art your dream company uses may prove yourself. "If the team doesn't like the way that you draw a dragon tail, even if it's an amazing drawing, then you won't get hired," Jeff from VonChurch explained.

Artists who can write a bit of code are always in hot demand as well. The automation skills can come in handy for mock-ups and other tasks.

Designers

As the name suggests, designers create the concept, storyline, and rules of a game. The role can be broken down into a variety of sub-disciplines, including world design, game writing, and level design. Once the core game components have been decided, some designers may double as engineers.

Designers are not necessarily expected to have an artistic back-ground, but they are expected to be highly creative. Recruiters typi-cally want people with some sort of development background, even if they won't be a full-time coder. Many schools offer courses or programs in game design, from which companies recruit designers.

Other Roles

Though development, production, art, and design may handle game creation, a number of other key support roles exist. The following are some of the most popular:

- **Quality assurance.** QA can be broken down into three types: functional testing, certification testing, and automa-tion testing. While automation testers usually need a com-puter science degree from a four-year university, the other two testing positions may require only a two-year degree. Testers need to have a high attention to detail, and testers-to-be should find a way to highlight this on their résumé. (*Note:* This would be an extremely bad time to make a spelling or grammar mistake.) Testers should understand the different permutations of a sequence of steps and should understand which ones to focus on in developing test cases. An under-standing of software can be handy here. QA tends to be faced with high turnover, as it's a relatively easy way into a gaming firm but is a nice avenue to other roles.

- **Customer support.** Requirements for a customer support agent tend to be less focused on academic or professional qualifications and more focused on one's "inherent" skills. A college degree may not be necessary at many companies, but candidates should have excellent verbal and written communication skills and a high attention to detail. Fluency in multiple languages is also highly desirable. Audra Aulabaugh from Big Fish Games advises candidates to see customer service roles as a way into a company. "We don't look for people to stay in this position forever. Come in, learn everything there is to know about our customer and our product, and then investigate other roles within the organization that are of long-term interest." A customer support agent can move on to roles like QA, partner relationships, and associate producer.

- **Marketing.** Marketing hires are divided across several disciplines requiring very different backgrounds. *In-game marketers* need to understand virality: how do games spread? What makes them popular? Successful candidates often have a quantitative background. *Business development marketers* build the partnerships that make games successful, and candidates often need an MBA to be considered for these positions. A background in mobile or online marketing is also useful.

Fresh Meat: Advice for College Candidates

A coworker of mine at Google had what one person described as the "Geek's Throwback Jersey": a Microsoft intern 1986 shirt. He wasn't especially old—just experienced. Much, much more experienced than I.

Social gaming, thus, has a delightful benefit for a recent college candidate: no one will have a 1986 internship shirt. Or even 2000. The field was essentially unheard of before 2005. The comparative newness of the field means rapid growth and plenty of room for promotions.

With that said, here is some additional advice for college students who are eager to break into this fast-growing field.

Don't Be Afraid of Entering Low

Customer support may not be the most glamorous use of your economics degree, but it's a great way to break into a fast-growing company. Or an English major might consider entering as a copywriter, with hopes of transitioning later to a marketing role. Financially and professionally, the company can matter more than the position.

In fact, recent college graduates can do very well at a social gaming company. "New grads can be great in positions close to the user, since they're much closer in age to the target market than more experienced employees," Alessandra (VonChurch) explained.

Joining a gaming company at any level will offer insight into the industry and help you establish contacts in the field. Then, when you want to "move up" to a new role, you'll have the credibility and relationships to do so.

Find Your Niche

While grads excited about gaming should join a company at any level they can get, they should try to develop a specialty as soon as possible. Jeff (VonChurch) reminds candidates that "they shouldn't get stuck in a less than ideal position for too long. Use the low entry point to explore positions, find a position you want to transition to, and do it."

Those who develop specialties will fare better in the long run as well. "It's about self-branding," Jeff says. "You build a name for yourself, and companies want to hire you for your specialty. It doesn't mean that you can't switch later, but people do tend to stay in their niche."

Create a Portfolio Web Site

While almost everyone could benefit from a portfolio/web site, this is especially important for artists and developers. Your portfolio or web site should list your résumé and projects you've done (including screenshots). A good portfolio will get your foot in the door, even without company experience.

Your résumé should also provide a link to your portfolio web site, and you should expect companies to check it.

Get Out There

Finally, because many smaller shops lack full college recruiting operations, it's especially important for such candidates to start building their name as soon as possible. Start networking. Join relevant Facebook and Meetup.com groups, and attend their sessions. Get an internship or take a part-time job. If you can't find a job for whatever reason, spend some time on your own, hacking together games.

Reaching Out and Getting In

"The best way in is if you have a contact," Jeff (VonChurch) says simply. While this is true of any technology company, it is especially true of smaller gaming companies. Software companies like Microsoft, Google, and Facebook can afford to scatter large masses of recruiters across the country to attend career fairs and meet candidates locally; the comparatively small casual gaming companies usually cannot. The three avenues below tend to be the most effective for establishing the personal connections that are critical to landing your job.

College and Professional Recruiting

Some larger companies may do some college recruiting, especially at the top universities. Even if you don't attend one of these universities, you may be able to pop over to one for a career fair. Just because a company doesn't recruit at your school doesn't mean it's unwilling to consider you; it may just mean that the company lacks the resources to recruit everywhere.

Alternatively, candidates with a bit of professional experience can consider working with a professional recruiting firm. As many gaming companies are small, this can be a great way to discover opportunities that may have otherwise escaped your notice.

Online Networks

LinkedIn's discussion groups are always a great avenue for recruiting, but Facebook should not be overlooked either. After all, many, if not all, of the companies you're recruiting for are *social* game companies. They quite literally live and die on Facebook. Becoming active in Facebook discussion groups about games or on a company's own page is a good way to get noticed. Rather than just asking for a job, consider first proving your worth. Offering insight and feedback will put you a step in front of all the other candidates banging at the door.

Similarly, become active in game developers' web sites and forums. If you are known as a person who helps others, you'll be seen as smart, skilled, *and* the kind of teammate everyone wants. Recruiters scour these forums for great candidates.

Events

Attending events in person can be one of the most effective ways to network. Recruiters will be able to see how you communicate and act, and to put a face to a name. This is (hopefully) a good thing.

The Game Developers Conference is a great chance for you to learn about the industry, and perhaps an even better opportunity for you to network. Recruiters flood the conference, as it acts as a huge recruiting event. Come with your "pitch" and business card ready. The registration fee is hefty, but college students can get access at a significantly reduced rate.

Additionally, if you follow companies on Facebook and Twitter, you may discover that they are hosting upcoming open houses, mixers, and happy hours. These events can be a great way to learn more about the company, meet current employees, or even network with attendees who work for other gaming companies.

Personality Fit

Geeks everywhere will be thrilled to hear that their personality doesn't matter—*too* much. Recruiters and hiring managers have resigned themselves to socially awkward developers. That's just what the field is like. As long as you're not arrogant and teammates wouldn't despise you, you're probably "good enough" on the personality front. However, while socialness is not required, "any engineer that that can carry on a conversation will be in high demand," said Katy Haddix, a recruiter at VonChurch.

For other positions, a strong personality fit is much more critical. These positions require more interfacing with coworkers, partners, and users. And, unlike for development positions, companies can afford to focus on the personality fit. The following five personality traits are some of the most universal requirements that interviewers will attempt to evaluate.

Some other traits, such as honesty and adaptability, are equally important but more challenging for an interviewer to assess. Demonstrating that you lack either of these, however, can certainly bar you from an offer.

Young at Heart

"You're working with teenagers," VonChurch recruiter Jeff says. "Sure, they may be technically 40 years old, but they're still teenagers."

Indeed, the casual gaming industry is young, in terms of the trade itself as well as the employees. This youthfulness gives it a high-energy, let's-go-grab-a-drink environment.

Additionally, Audra Aulabaugh from Big Fish adds, "The output is casual games. We want people who like to have fun because they're the ones who'll be able to build something really fun." Your suit-and-tie employee won't cut it there.

Console gaming companies are a bit more aged, but still cling to the young-at-heart culture.

Likable

Employees at casual game companies work unusually close with each other to push out their nearly monthly releases, and a so-called "bad apple" can be poisonous to a team environment. On top of this, you're working long hours many days, and when you're not, you're going to the bar, to happy hours, and the like. It's critical that you get along with your colleagues.

Confidence is good, but you need to check your ego at the door. There is nothing worse than a teammate who can't wait to tell you how superior he is. We've all met the type.

Creative / Imaginative

Even in roles that don't require an artistic flair, employees tend to be more creative and imaginative. This is reflected in everything from how they solve problems to their not-so-secret love for fantasy and sci-fi. Gaming companies will want to know that you are imaginative, as it's creativity that fuels their games.

Work Ethic

It's nice to be able to regurgitate the old line "it doesn't matter how many hours you work, as long as you get your work done," but the problem is that the work is never really done. Gaming companies require that you have the work ethic to put in these extra hours.

For this reason, a passion and drive for gaming and for the specific company is critical. You need to be willing to commit that time.

Strong Communication Skills

Cross-functional collaboration in order to rapidly push out a game is critical, forcing companies to stress strong communication skills. Interviewers want to see that you can explain and defend a position clearly, while also listening to and understanding another person's perspective. They may not ask as pointed questions to assess your communication skills as they might your technical skills, but you can bet they'll be evaluating it in every response. This is especially true if you want to move into a lead or management role.

The Gaming Interview—Three Tips to Doing Well

While all the standard interview advice (be concise, create questions to ask, etc.) applies equally to gaming advice, some advice is more specific to this field. The following three tips are especially important in gaming interviews, though they may be more broadly applicable as well.

1. Play the Game

Perhaps the best part of interviewing with a game company—other than getting a crack at giant version of the flagship games—is that your interview preparation *is* playing games. After all, you have to research any company before your interview. What better way to do that than to play its games?

While playing these games, be sure to think about the following questions:

- What are you impressed by?
- What makes it fun?
- What would you change in the next version?

In your answers to these questions, pay particular attention to anything that's relevant to your job title.

2. Show Confidence (but Not Too Much)

Because game companies move so fast, it's important that a candidate understand her skill set, and understand how it can be applied. "A candidate should be able to say 'I've done A, B, and C, and I know that I can do D,'" says Katy Haddix, a VonChurch recruiter. You need enough self-confidence to know that you can do something new, but not so much that you turn off your teammates.

3. Be Likable

Long hours make likability an essential trait, and even the least chatty person can apply a few tricks to make herself more sociable:

- **Smile.** Even if it's a phone interview, smiling will come through in your voice. In fact, not only does smiling make you appear happier, it actually makes you happier.
- **Laugh.** Laughing suggests to your interviewer that you like to have a good time and are fun to be around. Pay attention to how your interviewer acts, and mimic him. If he's more serious, then perhaps you should follow his lead.
- **Be agreeable.** Being a complete pushover won't help you in your interview, but you don't want to be argumentative either. You should assert your opinions while going out of your way to listen to your interviewer. Remember: *the interviewer is always right*. Stubborn candidates should make a special effort to keep this element under wraps.

However, while likability and sociability is important, that's no excuse for being unprofessional. Off-color comments have no place in an interview.

Your Questions Answered

Making the Jump

Dear Gayle,

I've been a back-end server programmer at Microsoft for several years now, and have no background in gaming. I really, really want to move to a gaming company, though. Will my lack of experience in gaming hurt me? What can I do?

~S. L.

Dear S. L.,

Sure, it'll hurt you, at least in the sense that all else being equal you'd fare better with some game programming. But you do have relevant skills, and you shouldn't forget that. Casual gaming companies do require server-side coding, and that just happens to be your specialty. Don't overlook that.

However, you'd stand a better shot if you did two things:

1. **Learn the necessary languages.** When you're applying to a company, they'll probably list a preference of languages. If not, you can probably track down some information online about what language they use. Learn them.
2. **Build a game.** Set aside a weekend or two to write a game. You'll get résumé-building experience, demonstrate a passion for games, and learn skills that will

(continued)

(continued)

> aid you in the interview. Provide a link or informa-
> tion on your résumé that the company can use to
> track down a copy of your game.
>
> And you might as well kill two birds with one stone—write
> the game in the language your top-choice company uses.
> ~Gayle

Value Added

> Dear Gayle,
> I've been attending some events hosted by gaming com-
> panies in order to start developing a network there, but I find
> I'm never getting what I want out of the events.
> The problem is that I don't know what to say to people. It
> feels awkward to "pitch" myself, and so no one even ends up
> discovering who I am and what I'm interested in.
> How can I make better use of my time?
> ~B. R.

> Dear B. R.,
> If it helps, try not thinking about the events as network-
> ing events. Try just approaching them as an opportunity to
> learn—the networking aspect will come.
> Prepare questions to ask people you meet in the industry.
> Stress that you don't know much about the industry but you're

interested in learning. When applicable, react to the questions
by sharing some of your own experiences:

You: What's the release cycle like at your company?

Them: We try to ship about every six to eight weeks, but
there are often delays. If we don't feel that the user
experience is quite right, we're not afraid of pushing
it back.

You: Oh, interesting. I work for Adobe, and we'll usually
try to cut features if it will help us meet a deadline. I
guess your approach makes more sense for the gaming industry, since you all don't have contracts with
businesses for specific deadlines. Since you ship so
frequently, though, how do you deal with software
updates? Do you just not do them since the issues will
be fixed in the next version?

As the conversation goes on, your companion will begin
to learn about what you do, and may even ask you for a
mini-bio.

To solidify this connection, create a reason to follow up
with the person ("I'd love to ask you some more questions
about the industry. Could I get your contact information?)—
and follow through on this. Empty promises won't help
you much.

~Gayle

It's the Little Things that Count

Dear Gayle,

When gaming companies ask me why I want to work there, I never know what to say. It sounds so trite to say something like "because I love games."

What makes a good response to this question?

~A. S.

Dear A. S.,

The key is in the details, but let's take a step back first. Why do companies ask this question?

There are two primary reasons: (1) they want to see if you've done your research, and (2) they want to know that you're interested and committed. Your job, therefore, is to give an answer that communicates both of those things.

Let's look at your answer from that perspective. Does it show that you've done your research? Not at all. Does it show that you're interested and committed? No, not any more so than the fact that you showed up.

So what would make a good answer? Something like this:

I've always valued my creativity, so gaming is a natural fit for my creative side as well as my drive to build cool things. I'm specifically excited about your company because I love its approach to fusing learning opportunities with fun. I saw a really interesting TED talk given by your CEO about the impact that engagement has in children's learning, and that really rang true for me.

Passion + Research = Excellence in Answering.

~Gayle

Chapter 11

The Offer

David and I met over drinks to discuss my job offer. This was negotiation number 3. I'd thought a more social atmosphere might relax the situation, but things didn't quite go as planned. David ordered just a glass of water—at a *wine* bar—and I couldn't help but note that his frugality with drinks seemed to fit so well with his lowball offer. Of course, if you talked to him, he'd tell you that the offer was more than generous.

We'd each appealed to higher authorities: David to the company's investors and to the Internet, and I to my super-CEO mother. The venture capitalists just shrugged and told him that it was his decision. The Internet gave him a conveniently decisive range for how much equity engineers get. My mother explained that "normal" ranges are meaningless; that it's a complex trade-off between salary, equity, vesting schedule, benefits, and job expectations. "Obviously, if your salary were a million dollars per year, you wouldn't need any equity." I couldn't disagree with her logic. Wine-is-too-expensive-for-me David could.

Ultimately, I had one thing on my side that he didn't: the word *no*. I could walk away, and my branding of an ex-Googler/Microsoftie/Applite would land me a new and equally exciting opportunity. David, however, had just cashed his check from the venture capitalists and desperately needed help getting his company off the ground.

Two more meetings and two more glasses of wine later (both mine, of course), we eventually struck a deal that was just good enough to satisfy our respective interests.

How to Evaluate an Offer

As my mother said, offers are complex. They include a salary, bonus, raises, vacation days, health care, and so on—and that's just the financial side. You also must consider your career direction, the company culture, your future teammates, and potentially even the feelings of a spouse or significant other. Then, to really muddy the waters, you rarely have all the information (How many hours will you be working? What are annual raises like?).

The complexities of an offer usually can be broken down into the following categories:

- **Career development.** Is this the right decision for your career? Will the job look good on your résumé? Will it help you progress in your career?
- **Financial package.** How much are they paying you? What are the perks (health care, stock, etc.) worth?
- **Happiness.** Will you enjoy the job? Will you get along with your teammates? Is the location where you want to live?

I can't tell you what the right decision is, but I can help you dissect an offer so that you can make the right decision *for you*.

Your Career Development

New candidate, same story: I accepted a job with <Insert Company Name Here> and I thought it was a great opportunity. And it was!

At first, anyway. But then, five years later, I was still at the same job, and I couldn't help but think—where had the prior year gotten me? I could have done something new or different, but instead I stayed at my job doing the same old stuff.

Technology companies especially are filled with people like this. Companies like Microsoft and Google are such great places to work that it's easy to lose sight of where you're going—and it's even easier to not want to jump ship.

I strongly recommend that, prior to accepting a job, a candidate map out her career path. You should know where you want your career to go, and what the path is to getting there. This will help you understand how to be successful in your career, as well as understand if a job is even right for you.

Learning and Development

Some companies have more rigorous training processes than others. Google, for example, sends every new employee through two weeks of "Noogler Training." These classes teach employees about Google as a company and take a deep dive into job-specific learning. Engineers, for example, will learn about BigTable, MapReduce, and other tools. This enables employees to understand what their colleagues outside of their team are doing.

In addition to new employee training, some companies may offer courses for continuing development, either within the company or at a local university. These courses can be incredibly valuable—or just a way of placating employees. Or, worse yet, they may say that they support their employees going back to school, but they may actually discourage it once you join. Don't take a company's word for it—ask to speak to an employee who has utilized these opportunities.

Responsibilities and Decision Making

As valuable as formal education is, you usually learn the most by doing. A position where you are given substantial responsibilities and are given the freedom to make mistakes will enable you to learn more powerful and relevant lessons.

In Peter's first two years as a software engineer at Google, he was given the opportunity to manage an intern, prepare design documents for key features, participate in planning and strategy discussions, and help shape the direction of the team. And all this was in addition to his regular responsibilities as a coder. When he left Google to join a start-up, he had no problems getting interviews for software engineering or program management positions. He had developed not only the technical skills necessary, but also the communication and planning skills.

To position yourself in the best possible way, look for teams that will give you responsibilities beyond your actual job description, and even beyond your level of responsibility. If you want to be a manager one day, look for teams that will let you mentor or manage someone—if it's "just" an intern. If you want to move from testing to development, find a position that will let you write code automation, and do periodic bug fixes.

Additionally, you should make sure you understand how decisions get made. Many companies love to say, "Oh, we make them as a team," but that's rarely the case. Who drives the decision? What happens when there's conflict? What decisions will you be responsible for, and what decisions do you merely offer feedback on?

Promotions

I have a rule: always go to a company (or team) that's growing. Growing companies means new employees and, hey, someone has to tell them what to do, right? And that person might just be me.

Even within more stagnant companies, though, there can be a wide range in one's ability to move up the corporate ladder. Ask about the following:

- **Tenure.** When is an employee considered a "new" employee? At a younger company, employees who have been there for just a year or two might be considered old-timers—though at Microsoft they would still be considered recent hires. Generally speaking, the shorter the tenure, the more opportunities there are.

- **Growth rate.** Don't be fooled by looking at the number of people that a company has hired each year. Huge companies like Microsoft hire thousands of people each year, but that doesn't mean the company is growing. The number you need to know is the *percent* growth. In the case of larger companies, the more relevant stat might be the growth of your team. After all, who cares if Bing is growing if you work on Windows?

- **Promoting from within.** Some companies promote from within, and some tend to hire senior positions from the outside. Intel, for instance, has a tradition of promoting internally. Google, however, hired many of their earlier managers externally. In this case, they had no other choice: the company was growing too rapidly, and the junior employees couldn't get ready fast enough to fill the management's shoes.

Résumé and Prestige

For better or for worse, having a big name on your résumé opens doors. It may not be the place where you would learn the most, or have the most responsibilities (though it might be), but it offers credibility that you won't get at a lesser-known firm. It's a stamp on your résumé that says, "I am at least *this* good."

Therefore, in considering an offer, be sure to analyze:

- **Company brand name.** How well known is the company? Remember that brand names are not universal. A company can have a strong brand within your field but not outside of your field, and vice versa. For example, working at the best advertising firm in the world may not help your résumé stand out when it's being reviewed by recruiters unfamiliar with advertising.

- **Position and title.** Some companies inflate titles, some companies deflate them, and others give titles that just aren't quite descriptive or appropriate. I've talked to a number of candidates from smaller companies who were officially "testers," but they actually spent their day writing production-level code. They can partially recover from this issue by listing both an official and unofficial title on their résumé, but they certainly would have been better off had they been listed as developers from the start.

Company's Future and Stability

Candidates frequently ask me questions like, "Is Microsoft stable? Will they do layoffs again?" I always respond with this question: "Well, what if they do?" I find that most candidates overemphasize the stability of a company.

If you find yourself trying to analyze the stability of a company, ask yourself what the (realistic) worst case is. You probably won't find yourself unable to find a job, kicked out of your apartment, and sitting on the streets of San Francisco with a sign saying, "Will Code for Food." More likely, you'll walk out with a few months of severance pay and you'll find a new job before you've even used that up.

That said, job stability may be quite important in certain cases. If you require a visa or hope to apply for a green card, layoffs could pose a serious threat to your life. Alternatively, if you have very specific skills or requirements in a job, finding a new job that is a good match could prove challenging. Only you can decide how much of a disruption layoffs could pose to your lifestyle.

Location

Amit, a soon-to-be PhD graduate, came to me with a dilemma. He was deciding between two offers: one from Intel in Santa Clara, and the other from AOL in Dulles, Virginia. He had been analyzing the financial package, the team, and the growth opportunities, but had skipped right over the location aspect.

"Amit," I asked him. "How long do you expect to stay at the company?" He told me that he would probably leave within several years. "OK, and then where will you go? What are your options?"

He had a three-year-old son and a four-year-old daughter. If he left AOL, he'd have a hard time finding a new job in the area. Dulles, Virginia, is not exactly a hotbed of a technology innovation. Leaving AOL would likely mean having to relocate and pluck his two young children out of their schools midyear and away from all their friends. Amit decided that dealing with two screaming young children would not make his job search much easier, and he decided to go to Intel.

Learn from Amit's lesson, and make sure to evaluate your future career opportunities in a location. Being trapped in a company is never a fun experience.

The Financial Package

We all know the old cliché "there's more to life than money," but my telling you this won't change your mind one bit. After all, you're the best person to decide how much money matters.

However, what I can tell you is that money is complicated. First, any differences in salary in the short term are likely to be dwarfed differences in your career opportunities. That is, if you learn a bunch at a company, you'll be able to get a higher-paying job down the road. Second, it can be tricky to understand which offer is the best paying.

In 2005, I faced this delightfully difficult decision: should I go to Google, Microsoft, or Amazon? Though I was dazzled by the money they were throwing at me, I had no idea who was paying the most.

Amazon had the lowest pay, but also offered a signing bonus and stock grants. Microsoft offered the highest salary, but offered only two weeks of vacation and virtually no stock. Google was somewhere in the middle on salary and offered options, and who knew what those would be worth? (This was, unfortunately, after they went public.)

And then, on top of it all, you had all the other perks and benefits: health care, free drinks, free lunch, and so on. Did those matter? And how much?

There's no precise formula to answer these questions, but there are some general guidelines to consider.

Components of an Offer

In additional to salary, offers from technology firms often consist of stock, bonuses, and other financial compensation. How do you compare offers that vary across multiple metrics? By putting a price tag on everything and dividing it by the number of years you expect to stay at the company.

For example, suppose Amazon offers you a $70k salary and a $20k signing bonus, and Google offers you a $4k signing bonus and $75k salary. Which company pays better? It depends on how long you expect to stay. If you expect to leave in two years, then Amazon pays better ($80k vs. $77k).

This means that the longer you stay at a company, the less these one-time perks matter.

To understand your financial compensation, you need to look at everything that's included in the offer, as well as things that aren't. Ensure that you have as many of the following as possible:

Core Offer Components	Other Financial Compensation
Salary	Typical annual bonus
Signing bonus	Typical annual raise
Relocation	Employee stock purchase plan
Stock options	401k plan (percent match and max contribution)
Stock grants	Health care, dental, and vision plans
Vacation	Additional perks: free food, etc.

Some of these factors, such as annual bonuses and annual raises, might be difficult to ascertain, as companies are reluctant to give out this information. If you can track down an employee, however, she might offer you an idea of what's normal versus what's good.

Location

Let's look at two hypothetical offers: Jason is offered $75k by Microsoft (Seattle, Washington) and $80k by Google (Mountain View, California). Google pays better, right? Wrong! California has a 10 percent state income tax, whereas Washington has a 0 percent state income tax. Google's $80k offer is really more like a $72k. And on top of that, Mountain View is, according to Payscale.com, about 25 percent more expensive than Seattle.

A dollar simply goes further in some areas. When comparing offers, make sure to take into account the location of the company by using cost-of-living calculators such as Payscale's.

The Happiness Factor

It's easy to look at a big, fat number in your offer letter and say, "Hey, I can stick it out a few years, right?" It's a lot harder to actually do that. Unhappy employees tend to work fewer hours, be less productive, and quit earlier.

Before taking a job where you suspect you'll be unhappy, think through whether you can really deal with it. Yes, you can handle long hours, if you like the work and your teammates. You might be able to deal with tasks you don't enjoy, if your coworkers are fun and the hours aren't terrible. But tedious work, long hours, frustrating coworkers, and a bad manager? It's a nightmare, and you're likely to quit so quickly or perform so poorly that you won't get much out of it, anyway.

What you need to figure out before applying to jobs (or at least before accepting a job) is the following: What makes you happy? Is it the people you work with? Is it being intellectually stimulated? Is it the feeling of accomplishment? Or impacting people's lives? It's easy to say "yes!" to all of these, so you should compare your answers to your previous jobs. Why were you happy or unhappy?

The following factors are important to many people:

- **Manager.** Your relationship with your manager is likely to be the most powerful influence on whether you enjoy your job. Make sure to have at least one conversation with your future manager and ask him questions like: What contributes to success at the company? What career paths have some of your prior employees taken? If possible, try to connect with these employees to discuss.

- **Teammates.** From credit stealers (people who take credit for other people's work) to outright nasty teammates, hostile coworkers are pervasive in many companies. They are almost always detrimental to your happiness—and why be miserable in a place where you spend half of your waking hours? Before accepting the offer, coordinate a time to grab lunch with your future team under the guise of "asking questions." They don't need to know that you're actually evaluating them.

- **Culture and environment.** Every company loves to say that they "just love to have fun" or "they have a culture of innovation," but come on—those terms are relative and can't describe every company. Ask your future coworkers how they would describe the culture, and ask for examples of this. If people can't offer illustrative examples of the culture they describe, it's a good sign that they're just regurgitating the company line.

- **Hours.** Depending on your stage in life and your general priorities, you may or may not be OK with working long hours. Regardless, it's important to know what you're getting yourself into. Discuss with your manager and your teammates what time they usually arrive at work and leave, and in what situations they need to work nights and weekends. Is it just before a major release, or is it on a more regular basis?

How Can You Negotiate an Offer?

You prepared thoroughly, you sweet-talked your way through résumé blemishes, and you mastered all the hard balls they threw at you. Finally, the offer comes and your mouth drops; it's thousands of dollars lower than what you'd hoped for. What can you do?

That depends on *what* you're trying to negotiate, and by *how much*. You probably can't argue your salary from $55k to $80k, but you might be able to persuade your recruiter to bump your salary up from $75k to match a competitor's $78k salary.

Should You Negotiate?

Most candidates, particularly recent graduates, don't negotiate their job offer. The reason? They're nervous. They've worked so hard to get the job, and they don't want to risk losing their offer.

Richard, a recruiter for Facebook, tells you not to worry. "Once we've decided to hire you, we're going to do everything we can to do that. A little negotiating will not hurt you."

So go ahead and discuss your concerns with your future company. As long as you're polite and respectful of the recruiter's time, no one will fault you for negotiating.

What Can You Negotiate?

Virtually any part of your offer *can* be negotiated—after all, rules are made to be broken, but some are much harder than others. Vacation time, for instance, is usually quite rigid because it's so visible. When companies state exactly how many vacation days are awarded for each year at the company, it's difficult to bend the policy, even for exceptional candidates.

Some of the easiest (and most commonly negotiated) terms are salary, stock options or grants, relocation, and the signing bonus. Stock options are often the most flexible, since their exact value can be relatively hard to quantify and can fluctuate too often to have rigid HR policies. One candidate, Amy, convinced Google in 2004 to double her stock options. Though she had no idea of their actual value at the time, she became very thankful a few months later when the company completed its initial public offering (IPO).

Sometimes, negotiation is more about changing the terms—in a way that may be neutral to the company but positive to you—rather than truly improving a term in an absolute sense. For example, Microsoft offers a wonderful relocation package where movers pack up all your stuff, transport it to Seattle, and unpack it in your new location. As nice as this is, you might prefer just to enlist friends to help with moving and take the cash instead. Many college candidates have done just this, and walked away $5,000 richer. After all, they didn't really want to keep that old futon with the beer stains.

Seven Tips to Winning Negotiations

When you get an offer, the first thing you should do is to thank the company for their time and to reiterate that you are confident that you can do an excellent job. The second thing you should do is open the negotiations. Following these tips will ensure more positive results:

1. **Don't name the first number.** The first person to name a number can overshoot too much and turn off the other person ("He offered that?!? What's the point in even discussing it!"), or, even worse, might lowball himself. Whenever possible, avoid giving the recruiter a salary range by saying that there are many factors you evaluate in a job and that it's difficult to provide a range. You may even be able to tactfully avoid giving your prior salary by stating that your company does not permit disclosure of salaries.

2. **Have a viable alternative.** You can claim that you are really excited about doing system administration for your brother's company, but Google probably won't buy it. However, if you tell Google that Microsoft is offering you $5k more, you can bet that Google will feel much more threatened that they'll lose you. Also, don't forget to take location into account. It's perfectly reasonable to tell Google that while their salary is $1,000 higher than Microsoft's, it's effectively much lower with the cost-of-living difference.

3. **Do your research.** By being armed with data about industry salary and what your company offers to similar candidates, you'll have a much better idea of what is reasonable to ask for and what isn't. Check out web sites like Glassdoor.com to research salary ranges.

4. **Have a specific "ask."** If you ask a recruiter for just "more salary," they're likely to bump up your salary by an insignificant amount, putting you in the uncomfortable position of needing to ask *again*. Instead, you should approach your recruiter with specific demands: salary of $X, signing bonus of $Y, and so on.

5. **Overshoot.** The salary that you request acts as a ceiling: the most a company would have to pay you for you to accept their offer. A recruiter is likely to shoot for somewhere between

the initial offer and what you ask for, so you should overshoot by a bit. But don't go overboard; asking for a $200k salary in your first year out of college just makes you come across as unreasonable.

6. **Use your best medium.** Many people will insist that negotiations take place over the phone. If you're comfortable doing so, then by all means, pick up the phone and call the recruiter. But if you're not—if you think you might get bullied into accepting a subpar offer—then stick to e-mail, where you can tweak every word.

7. **Sell yourself.** Though you've gotten the offer, you need to continue to sell yourself. A recruiter who thinks you're working with them (rather than just griping about every penny), who enjoys your personality, and who thinks that you'll add value to the company will do more to get you there.

And remember: if and when the company agrees to your terms (or you to theirs), the negating is done. You cannot go back and ask for more. You should tell them how excited you are to join them, and always, always ask for the offer in writing.

Tricky Issues: Deadlines, Extensions, and Declining Offers

How you communicate with your recruiter or manager is a sign of your professionalism. Are you cognizant of the time and effort they spend recruiting, or do you think that recruiting is all about you? By being open with your recruiter about your other pending offers and your feelings about the job, you can avoid catching her off-guard. Recruiters just *hate* surprises—or at least they hate bad ones anyway.

Deadlines and Extensions

When Amazon first offered me a job, I was given one week to decide. The problem was that I was still mid-interview with Google and Microsoft. I explained to them the reality: I could not make a decision without all the options in front of me. And guess what? They waited for four weeks, until I finally turned Amazon down in favor of Google.

Companies give deadlines for a good reason; they can't effectively interview candidates while holding open a position for you, nor do they want to drag out a decision for too long. Within reason though, they will negotiate with you to extend the deadline.

If you need an extension, simply be up front with the recruiter. Explain to him *why* you need an extension, *what* your status is with other companies, and *when* you'll be able to have a decision ready:

Hi Samantha,

I noticed that you had given me a deadline for this offer of the 16th. I'm a bit concerned about my ability to meet that. While I'm very excited about Microsoft, I of course feel it's important to have all my options in front of me before making a decision. I'm sure you can understand that.

I'm currently in the process of interviewing for Google, and I've asked my recruiting contact there to expedite the decision as much as possible. I will interview with Google on the 14th, and I hope to hear back by the 20th. I believe I'll be able to make a decision quickly thereafter.

Could we push back the offer deadline until the 25th?

Thank you,

~Gayle

Note that I didn't just say that I need an extension, but I also gave the recruiter my status with Google. The reason for this is that she may know much more about Google's process than I do. She may know, for example, that it's difficult for Google to make a decision within a week.

In smaller companies or companies with very specific openings, extending a deadline substantially may be more difficult. Companies like Google or Facebook, where your offer doesn't come from a specific team (and thus you're not blocking their recruiting) are more likely to be amendable to extensions.

Reneging

The common advice is "never, ever renege," and, well, I hate to argue with that. They're right, more or less. Reneging is somewhat unethical and, frankly, should rarely come up. After you accept an offer, you should reject all future interview requests. You shouldn't even be in a position to be tempted.

But things happen. Sometimes a company that previously rejected you comes back with a spontaneous offer. And it's just too good to turn down. Then what? Then you have a very difficult decision to make.

In fact, that's exactly what happened to me. Just before my last year of college, I interviewed for internship positions at Apple and IBM. Apple rejected me, so I accepted IBM's offer. I was just lukewarm toward IBM, but I didn't want to go back to Microsoft for a fourth summer, so I accepted IBM's offer. Three months later, Apple came back and offered me the position. Apparently, their number one candidate reneged, and I was number two.

Perhaps I should have turned it down and taken the "high road," but I was just too excited about the position to do that. My IBM recruiter was furious (probably more so after offering her a lame excuse about my sick grandmother), but they found a replacement—a girl who probably reneged on her offer with another company. I'll never know how far this reneging chain goes.

The guy who reneged on Apple (to go to Microsoft) took a much more honest approach; he told Apple about the Microsoft offer (which was apparently unusually high), and they were supportive of him accepting the other offer. He never needed to worry about bumping into his Apple interviewers years later, because they knew what had actually happened.

In an ironic twist of fate, I met this guy three years later in an interview room at Google. I didn't know his name previously, but the candidate's "how I got to Microsoft" story sounded so eerily similar that I made the connection.

So, no, I don't think that reneging is always and absolutely the wrong thing to do. After all, the decision impacts you far more than the company. But it should be taken very, very seriously. It can damage your reputation, your school's reputation, or your friend's reputation if he/she referred you. And, of course, it hurts the company itself. Think long and hard before doing this, and avoid taking any more interviews once you've accepted an offer.

Declining an Offer (and Building a Connection)

Turning down an offer does not mean severing contact; it should be viewed more as "taking a rain check." Think of it this way: you liked the company enough to go through the full recruiting process, and they liked you enough to give you an offer. This is a connection you definitely want to maintain.

You should turn down the offer in whatever medium you've been using for communication and with whomever you've been corresponding the most. That is, if the recruiter has been calling you regularly, you should decline the offer over the phone with him. Alternatively, if you've been e-mailing your manager the most, you should decline the offer first to the manager over e-mail. You should follow up these correspondences with short e-mails or phone calls to whoever else you've talked with frequently.

In your e-mail or phone call, use these tips to avoid burning bridges and to strengthen your relationship:

- **Be polite and professional.** No matter how tense the prior negotiations have gotten, you should always address your recruiter in a nice and respectful way. Some people may be particularly upset about your declining the offer, after spending so much time and money on you, but don't let this bother you. Be open and understanding, but stand firm in your decision.

- **Provide a non-negative and non-negotiable reason.** Saying that the company is "too bureaucratic" is insulting, but saying that you would "prefer a smaller company at this point in time" is not. You should make sure that these reasons are not things the company could provide (such as a different location, if the company has only one location) or be prepared to reopen negotiations if they do. When declining over the phone, you should be prepared to say what offer you have accepted and why.

- **Ask to stay in touch—and mean it.** Close your e-mail to the recruiter or manager with a note expressing a desire to stay in touch. You can follow up a day or two later with a LinkedIn connection. If you have friends or colleagues who might be interested in the position, ask the recruiter if they'd appreciate some referrals from strong candidates that you know. You'll probably be doing your friend, and the recruiter, a favor. And it's a great way to stay in everyone's good graces!

Your Questions Answered

Au Revoir, Vacation Days

Dear Gayle,

I've been planning a three-week trip to Europe for over a year—dates set, flights booked, etc. The issue is that I'm now applying for a new job and, if I get it, I'll be expected to start about six weeks before my trip. I obviously won't have built up enough vacation time by then to take this trip. How do I handle this?

~T. K.

Dear T. K.,

The appropriate time to inform the company of your preplanned vacation is when you get the offer—not before, not after.

If you mention it before, you run the risk of the company's using this as an easy way to ding you in favor of another candidate.

If you mention this after you accept the offer, then you run the risk of the company's balking at your request and either refusing the vacation time or at the very least being nasty to you from day one.

Situations like this come up more than one might expect, and they're usually easily accommodated. Just before you accept, send your primary contact an e-mail explaining the situation as follows:

I'm really excited about joining your company.

(continued)

(continued)

Before I accept the offer, I do need to inform you of one potential complication. I've had a three-week trip to Europe (from DATE to DATE) planned for over a year. I recognize that this trip is at an inconvenient time—just six weeks after my proposed start date—but, unfortunately, the dates aren't flexible.

Is there some way to accommodate this? I'd be happy to do whatever you think is best—take unpaid time off, go "negative" on vacation days, etc.

Thank you!

Most likely, the company will just have you go "negative" and you'll have to be very conservative with vacation days to earn them back. Once you work things out with your primary contact and sign your offer letter, you should inform anyone else who needs to know. It would be an ugly surprise to your manager to discover this trip in your first few days.

In the event that the company refuses to accommodate your vacation time, you may be able to appeal to your secondary contact (if any).

~Gayle

Representative Representatives

Dear Gayle,

People always say that "you're interviewing the company just as much as they're interviewing you," and that's where my question comes in.

I finished a full round of on-site interviews and enjoyed the experience as much as one could. The potential future coworkers seemed nice enough, smart enough, etc. It was the HR people I didn't like.

My first phone screen was with a woman from HR whom I just didn't mesh with. She was basically reading off a script and seemed to barely register a lot of my responses. When she responded with anything other than an "OK," it was to argue with my answer. I guess I did well enough though, to keep going.

When I came on-site, I met with a different person from HR—this time a man—and I again felt it was a somewhat hostile interaction. There was none of that friendliness that I'm used to seeing from recruiters. He talked with me for all of about five minutes when I came, and then made me sit in a chair outside his office for over 30 minutes until my first interviewer came to get me. When I asked him where I could get a drink of water, he actually seemed annoyed that I would disturb his precious time.

But it's a good job, and I liked my actual coworkers enough. Should I let this bother me?

~E. B.

Dear E. B.,

I'd definitely look into the situation more. You have raised some valid red flags, but there are a few explanations.

1. **You got unlucky.** Maybe there are only two bad recruiters in the entire group of 30+ recruiters, and you happened to get them.
2. **It's symptomatic of a bad culture.** You didn't say that you *loved* the people—just that they seemed fine. Maybe things really are bad under the hood.
3. **The recruiters are too busy.** The actions of both of your recruiters could be explained by a very under-staffed HR department.

(continued)

(continued)

- Reading off a script → tired.
- Not responding → preoccupied.
- Arguing = well, some arguing is OK.
- Making you wait for 30 minutes → busy.

It could really be any of these, which means that you need to do some investigating.

Try to get to know your future team a bit better—join them for lunch or chat with them on the phone. Make sure to talk to multiple team members, as liking just one is far from representative. If you develop a particularly strong rapport with one, you could even delicately broach the subject. ("I've really enjoyed getting to know everyone here. I was a bit worried, to be honest, because of some things that happened during the recruiting process, but I've had such positive interactions since then.") If they bite, then you could explain the situation. Stick to the facts and avoid blaming anyone.

Alternatively (or additionally), you could find some other sources. Check with your friends to see if anyone has a contact at the company. Or, if it's a big enough company, you might be able to find some information about the culture online. Remember, though, there's a vocal minority and it's usually negative. Take things with a grain of salt.

~Gayle

Big or Little

Dear Gayle,

   I need some career advice. I'm graduating from college, and I'm trying to decide between two offers. One is from my friend's

start-up—I'd be employee number four—and the other is from
Amazon. I keep going back and forth. What should I do?
~L. R.

Dear L.R.,

Here is my humble advice: spend one year at Amazon, and
then go to your friend's start-up—unless, of course, you think
the start-up opportunity is a once-in-a-lifetime opportunity.

Let me explain.

Start-up opportunities will come by all the time. Trust
me. Even if you have no interest in ever working at a start-up,
you'll still have people banging on your door asking you to
join them. You aren't giving up your chance to go to a start-
up, you're just delaying it.

When you turn down Amazon's offer, you're giving up a
lot. You're giving up the "you're good" nod people will give
when they see your résumé. You're giving up the opportunity
to learn how "real" software development (with code reviews,
style guidelines, and all that) works. And you're giving up the
chance to get a "freebie" pass to quit a job after a short amount
of time. No one will think it's funny that a college hire quit his
Big Company job to go to Little Company after just a year.
Joining Big Company for just a year a bit later in your career
will look a bit odd.

So, unless your friend's start-up is the next Facebook,
you should go to Amazon. All you need is a year, and then you
can freely leave.

~Gayle

Chapter 12

On the Job

If it feels like the interview cycle never stops, that's because it doesn't. You need to start thinking about your next career jump on your first day at the current job. What will you do? When will you switch positions? Will you stay at your company or go to a new one?

Most new employees are extremely focused on creating great work, but that's only half the battle. To get promoted or get a nice, fat raise, you do (hopefully) need to execute on your responsibilities very well. But you also must build strong relationships, understand your weaknesses, and position yourself to make important accomplishments for the company.

Additionally, you need to know where you want to go to next. What's the point in slaving to become the best darn software engineer you can be if you want to become a program manager?

Your Career Path

The first year that Christine joined Amazon, she was thrilled. Great team. Great pay. And a company that most people would kill to work for. The second year was the same, as was the third and fourth year. She loved it there. Why would she leave? The dramatic rise of the stock price didn't hurt either.

By year five, she was finally ready for a change and started shopping her résumé around. She realized then what far too many people do: she didn't really need those extra few years at Amazon. She could have just left after two years and been in almost the same position. Oops.

It's easy to get sucked into a big company and let the years fly by blissfully unaware. This is why it's important to map out your career early and to check in on it often.

Define Your Career Path

Having a written career path will ensure that you understand, up front, how long you intend to be at a company and what you believe you'll get out of it. Your plans may change, of course, either because you can actually move faster than you had originally thought or because your goals changed. In that case, simply redefine your career path.

Your career path will force you to rethink that extra year: are you really going to get something new out of the job? It will also highlight what background you need to make the next jump.

Your plan should stretch at least 7 to 10 years in the future.

Depending on your manager and your field, you could consider sharing your desired path with your supervisors (or at least a tweaked one expressing interest in moving up at the company). Your supervisors will be in an excellent position to help you acquire the desired experience.

Make Your Successes Known

No one likes a person who gloats about everything they've done, but at the same time, you won't advance if people don't know about

When:	2 years	1 year	1-2 years	2+ years
What:	Software engineer at major company	Software engineer at start-up	Program manager/director at (hopefully) same start-up	MBA at top-tier school
What I need:	CS degree Project experience Prior internships	Professional coding experience.	Some leadership experience Strong technical back-ground Passion for start-up	Substantial leadership Extra-curriculars Prior successes
What I will get:	Gain credibility from big name Improve coding skills Learn about profes-sional software	Start exploring related options Get involved with less technical decisions Connections and cred-ibility within start-up community	Develop leadership skills and project management skills Learn about fund-raising, marketing, and other areas of business Oversee at least three people	Expand network across United States Develop credibility Improve business background
Notes	Need to develop start-up network within first year, and begin looking for appropriate start-up within second year	Be clear with company from beginning that I want to be exposed to noncoding problems	Develop extracurriculars Expand network outside of company	If decide to pursue MBA, find outside (volunteer, etc.) activities

your successes. Here are a few tactics to publicize your accomplishments without turning off your teammates:

- **Send your manager regular updates.** Keith from Google e-mails his manager an update before their regular one-on-one meetings. "I describe what I've accomplished in the past week and what problems I experienced doing so. This not only helps to make our meetings more efficient, but it also helps to create a record each week of what I've accomplished. This comes in handy during review time," Keith says.
- **Set team goals (and update them).** Encourage your team to set weekly goals, and send a weekly e-mail with the team's progress. This will allow you to highlight your progress, in addition to that of the rest of your team.
- **Applaud your teammates.** Doing well does not mean your teammates have to do poorly. In fact, if you go out of your way to publicly praise your teammates, they are less likely to feel competitive or angry when you mention yours.

The common theme is to have a *reason* to mention your progress. No one likes someone who shows off for no reason, and getting too close to this will inflame the competitive spirit of your teammates.

Managing the Review Process

Many people have a love/hate relationship with the semiannual reviews. We understand that companies have to do them, and we may even look forward to them, as they're our chance to get promoted. But, still, we get slapped with so-called constructive criticism, and we have to write extensive comments about everything we've done over the past six months to a year.

Additionally, reviews are inevitably biased toward your most recent work since that's freshest in people's minds. To make the most of the review process, try the following tips.

1. *Track Your Accomplishments as You Go*

If you've decided to e-mail your manager with your weekly progress, then great! You may not even need to do this at all. Otherwise, it may help to have an easily accessible file where you list your biggest accomplishments.

When one task is more or less wrapped up, write up your review-ready blurb right then and there. You'll be able to remember all the details, hardest parts, and lessons learned much better than you will after several months have passed.

If you've been storing this file on your work computer and you leave the company, consider taking this file with you. You'll want it for your résumé or for your interview preparation.

2. *Quantify the Results*

Much like on your résumé, you will also want to quantify your accomplishments for your review. The earlier you collect this information, the better. Imagine how much better a statement like "implemented performance improvements, resulting in a 17 percent reduction in costs" sounds than a vague statement like "implemented performance improvements." If you can't quantify the result, then you should at least record any impact or comments people had.

3. *Ask Early for Feedback—and Get It in Writing*

After I was blindsided by a midsummer internship review at Microsoft, my HR representative encouraged me to ask for more feedback, and to do so more regularly. That was the last thing I wanted to do, but I did as she'd advised. In fact, I asked my mentor every two weeks for feedback.

Good news—I was doing great! I had corrected the one "issue" from my midsummer review (not submitting my code often enough), and I was clearly on track to get an offer at the end of the summer.

My final review started off just as I had expected. My mentor, with whom I worked the most closely, discussed all the great work

I did, and had little to no negative comments. I was thrilled. Then came my manager's section: I would not be getting an offer for three reasons. First, I had missed key deadlines. Second, my code had "several significant bugs." Third, I was not sufficiently boastful about my work.

I was stunned. This directly contradicted my mentor's continuous feedback and review comments, as well as my office mate's comments.

Thanks to my HR manager's earlier advice, I had the data to fight this. I appealed to a higher authority—the hiring manager—and told him what had happened. I had no interest in rejoining the team after this experience, but company policies dictate that if "your" team doesn't give you an offer, you can't reinterview for a year.

I'll never know what my manager's issue with me exactly was (though I have my theories), but he quickly backed down. It turned out he'd be happy to see me back at the company—just not on his team. Hmm. Well, that was just fine with me.

The constant feedback from my mentor saved me. I knew exactly how I was performing at all times. Had I not known that, I might have acquiesced to the unreasonable feedback.

Constant feedback will also enable you to correct issues early on, before they come up in your performance evaluation. And they're likely to be more reliable, as other evaluations will apply more weight to recent events.

Play a Bit of Politics: Build Strong Relationships

We may hate the office politics, but what can you do? They're a fact of life. In order to get ahead, people need to like you, or, depending on the position, at least respect you. This is especially true if you hope to be promoted to a team lead or manager position.

Being well liked doesn't mean you need to be Mr. or Ms. Popular. You don't have to slick your hair back into a pretty blond ponytail and wear a short cheerleader's skirt (in fact, please don't).

Being well liked just means being a great team player. Make an effort to do the following:

- **Help others.** Chip in to help the new guy, or discreetly help a struggling coworker. It'll earn the respect and appreciation of others.
- **Be supportive and positive.** Good moods are infectious. Keeping a smile on your face and being positive about changes in the team or company will make people want to be around you. Plus, no one will really want to bad-mouth the guy who's nice to everyone.
- **Give credit.** When a coworker does something impressive, be the one to shoot out an e-mail to the team congratulating her. Or if people praise you for something where the applause really should be shared, make a point of acknowledging your partner's help. You may be downgrading your own work to a small degree, but such kindness will easily be repaid.
- **Appeal to egos.** Everyone wants to feel important and valued; give your coworkers what they want here. Show them that you want to learn from them and that you think they're smart and insightful (even when you're not so sure).
- **Shut up and listen.** Sometimes, we disagree with our coworkers so strongly that we want to scream. In these cases, the best thing you can do is to just listen. This will show them that you understand their perspective and that you value it. They'll likely return the favor by listening to you.

Those with strong relationships are not only perceived better, but they also tend to be more effective performers because they know how to get team support.

Identify a Mentor

A mentor is more than just someone who can teach you—she is also your advocate. Just like a parent wants to see his child succeed, a leader wants to see her protégé succeed.

Seek out a mentor who has the following traits:

- **Successful.** While your peers can, of course, give you good advice as well, you'll generally get better advice from someone who is 5 to 15 years ahead of you. Less than 5 years and they won't have too much wisdom; more than 15 years and they're likely to be out of touch with your issues.
- **Similar goals.** Advice from people who are successful in very different fields is likely to be unhelpful at best, and detrimental at worst. What do you think the successful entrepreneur will tell you about your goal to be a VP at Microsoft? Probably something about bureaucracy and how you can't ever really effect change. Maybe he's right, maybe he's not, but that's hardly helpful if that's your goal. People with similar goals are likely to understand what did and didn't work for them, and will also be able to relate the experiences of their peers to you.
- **Similar background.** Your prior background will heavily affect your ability to accomplish your goals. Someone who went to a far stronger, or weaker, school, is unlikely to be able to tell you how to leverage or handle your school's name. Seek out those with a similar education and career background, as their struggles will probably closely match you.
- **Supportive, encouraging, and trustworthy.** Your mentor is not just there to offer advice; she is also there to encourage you. A good mentor will enable you to open up about your concerns and will help to ease them. She'll be supportive of you, whether you fail or succeed. And, of course, you need

to be able to trust her to be honest with you when there's something negative you need to hear.

- **Has time for you.** Though this should be obvious, it's often overlooked. Your mentor needs to have the time for you. What's the point of a mentor if they're never there to chat or to connect you with the right resources?

If you read through the preceding five points, you'll note that what you're essentially looking for is someone who's just like you, only a few steps ahead. And that's a good thing, even if it's difficult for some people to find. If you can't find the "perfect" mentor, that's OK. There's no reason you can't have multiple mentors.

Many people ask me if managers can be mentors. The answer is that, like most things in life, it depends. Your manager can certainly serve as a mentor in many ways, but you can't necessarily trust him to be unbiased. His first priority is to your company, not to you. If you're a star performer, will he really encourage you to leave, even if that's what's best for your career?

Promotions and Raises

Annual and semiannual reviews are not just a time to get feedback; they're also a time to get promoted or get a raise—or both. To position yourself effectively for these opportunities, you'll want to think ahead and to carefully craft your own evaluation to make it clear that you deserve the boost.

How to Get Promoted

Many companies, including Microsoft and Google, have some system of "career levels," enabling an employee to get promoted without a title or any other substantial change. Microsoft, for example, utilizes a universal level system, where employees enter at a level (usually between 58 and 65), depending on their prior experience and their new title. A promotion might constitute moving from a level 60 to a 61. Google uses a somewhat similar system, but instead assigns engineers to titles like Software Engineer I, II, or III (and then on to Staff or other titles). Moving from one title to the next may not change your work much if at all.

Such companies (as well as many other companies) tend to have well-defined metrics for what attributes an employee at a particular level should exhibit. These may be written in a formal document, but if not, have a discussion with your manager.

By examining the attributes you need to have, you can make sure to acquire the relevant skills or just demonstrate that you have them. If the next level up requires being able to lead key feature design, then ask your manager to let you take on some of these responsibilities. The earlier you plan for promotion, the better.

And remember, it's usually easiest to get promoted when you show that you're already performing at that next level.

How to Negotiate a Raise

In many ways, getting a raise is tougher than getting a promotion. At least a promotion, even if it includes a raise as well, involves your asking for something more in exchange for contributing more to the company. A raise, however, just means that the company is paying you a bit more and they get little else additional out of it—except, of course, a reduced chance that you'll leave.

Companies understand that raises are a part of doing business and, by following a few suggestions, you can increase the chances that you'll get your much deserved raise.

Choose the Right Time

There are better times and worse times to request a raise, and in the middle of tough times for your company is probably not one of them. It may, in fact, have a detrimental effect, as it calls attention to just how much (or how little) you are worth.

The ideal time to ask for a raise is when things are going well for your company *and* its competitors. A company's primary motivation in giving you a raise is to ensure that you stick around. If they can't afford your raise, or if there's little risk of your leaving, you're unlikely to get it.

Additionally, you should ask for a raise when it's convenient for your boss. After all, even if he wants to grant it to you, it may not be his decision. You need to ensure that he has the time and energy to go out and fight for you. If he's busy with other projects, or he's fighting for approval on other things (particularly things that increase your team's financial cost), he may not be a great advocate for you.

Do Your Homework

Because a company's primary motivation in giving a raise is to prevent you from leaving, you'll have a much better case if you can show that you're underpaid. Web sites like Payscale and Glassdoor.com can be useful tools in assessing how your pay compares with the industry pay. Be careful, however, in relying too heavily on that. Both web sites rely on averages that users submit in exchange for getting something else. Users may rush through it and provide inaccurate information. Many people have found that this data does not match up with their own experience.

It may be more useful to ask your friends, or even very trustworthy coworkers, for their salary information. People are surprisingly open about their salary if they can trust you and if they understand why you're asking.

How to Ask

Your request for a raise should be backed up with solid reasons, and "Sally needs braces" is not a reason. Reasons include your accomplishments and what you've done for the company. If you can quantify your contributions in a dollar amount, that's even better. What company wouldn't fight to retain someone who was contributing millions to the company?

If you have coworkers who have been through this process and that you can confide in, you may want to consider asking them for their advice. They may be able to direct you on what people actually value or don't value. This may be different from what the company states publicly. For instance, many companies state that they value employees mentoring new employees. The company likely recognizes that mentorship is important in general, but this doesn't mean that it's strongly weighted during the performance evaluation process.

Finally, much like in the offer negotiation process, you should shoot for more than what you can realistically expect. The company is more likely to meet you in the middle than to give you everything you ask for.

How to Handle Rejection

Your boss said no? Don't despair—that's common. Instead of just walking out of her office, ask her what would need to change to get the promotion or raise. Is it the company's financial situation? Do you need to take on more leadership responsibilities? What specifically would that entail?

Follow up this conversation with an e-mail summarizing this information. Then, the next time you ask for a promotion or raise, you can cite how you've done everything she's asked for.

If the issue is that the company simply can't afford it, consider alternative ways that the company could reward you. Perhaps they could let you work from home one day per week?

Finally, if your chances of getting a promotion or raise look poor for the foreseeable future, perhaps you should consider finding a new position—outside the company. What's the point of sticking around if there are no additional rewards for you?

How and When to Quit

Once upon a time, people got a job and stuck with it for nearly their entire lives. But now, much to the chagrin of the older generation, this fierce loyalty has been replaced by an expectation that you have at least two or three jobs by age 30. Stick around too long and you may be considered "tainted" by that company's culture.

I don't subscribe to that theory, personally, but I do think many people stick around at early companies for longer than is productive. If your goal is to move up into senior management at that company (or even a similar company), then by all means, stay. Otherwise, you might want to look into leaving earlier, and this where this advice comes in.

Should You Quit?

People quit for a few main reasons: (1) to change/improve their career path, (2) higher pay elsewhere, or (3) unhappiness.

If your goal in leaving is to find a place where you're happier, it's worth considering other options within the company. For example, if you have a bad boss or frustrating coworkers, you might be able to move to a new team. If you are bored, you might want to ask for additional responsibilities or to switch positions within the company.

Remember that there is value in sticking with the same company. Not only are frequent job hoppers looked down upon (read: you only get so many short stints on your résumé before companies get concerned), but it's usually easier to switch roles within the same company than to switch companies and positions. When you transition roles within one firm, you have already built trust and the firm understands your relevant skills at a great depth. Trying to switch positions at firms is much harder.

How to Not Burn Bridges

If you've ever had a job you hated, you've probably dreamed of quitting in some epic way. A public memo citing everything your boss did wrong. Spelling "I Quit" with spaghetti on the cafeteria floor. Borrowing the most annoying children of your friends to run wild around the office. It would be refreshing and—hopefully, I don't need to tell you this—incredibly stupid.

Even if you don't intend to have some massive blowout quitting ceremony, your departure is still likely to be a sensitive time, and it's all too easy to burn bridges. It's too small a world out there to do that; you may need your coworkers for references, or you might even end up working with them down the road.

To avoid leaving a foul taste in their mouths, do the following:

- **Give sufficient notice.** Two weeks is considered a bare minimum, but depending on the importance of your role and the situation, longer might be appropriate. At a small company, extra time may be appropriate due to the difficulty of finding someone to fill in.
- **Find an appropriate time.** Leaving halfway through a project or just before a deadline should be avoided, where possible. Ideally, you should leave as a project ends or even right when a project is beginning.
- **Voice concerns early.** If you're leaving because of specific things about the company you don't like, particularly if these are changeable, voice these concerns early. It's in your best interest to give your boss a chance to fix things.
- **Tell your manager first.** As tempting as it may be, don't tell anyone that you're leaving until your manager knows. It could get very ugly if he hears it from someone else first.
- **Leave on a positive note.** Work extra hard in your final days to make sure that your work is wrapped up or at least passed on to an appropriate person. You'll be remembered fondly for putting in the additional effort.

If you're leaving to go to a direct competitor, you should be aware that you might be walked out immediately without being given the chance to finish out even two weeks. During my time in Google's Seattle office, where many of the hires came directly from Microsoft, I would estimate that about half of them were escorted off the premises the day they gave their notice. Take a lesson from them and have your desk *discreetly* cleared out before you talk to your manager.

Should I Find a New Job First?

When I left Google, I didn't know exactly what I was going to do next. People thought I was crazy to not have a specific job lined up. I wasn't. I wanted to take several months to travel, work a bit on some side projects, and then find a start-up to join. Eventually. Once I found one I liked enough. I was in no rush.

There are some downsides, of course, to not finding a job first. First, you may lose some negotiating leverage if you're desperate for a job. Second, you might not be able to afford taking several months off without pay, and you may therefore get pressured into taking a mediocre new job. Third, if it takes you unexpectedly long to find a new job, extended unexplained gaps in your résumé can look suspicious.

However, looking for a job once you're unemployed has its perks. Namely:

- **No pressure.** If you're unhappy at your current job, you may be pressured to take something—anything—else. Once you've left, you don't need to be in any rush to find something new. After all, a job means no more vacation.
- **Search openly.** Once you've left, you can publicly post to Facebook, Twitter, your blog, or wherever, that you're looking for a new job. There's no need to hide your job search from your friends, or even your (former) coworkers, and some might know about the perfect position for you.

- **Extended vacation.** No more worrying about using up your precious 15 days of paid time off. Now you can take that extended vacation to Europe (or, in my case, South America).
- **Unlimited time.** Interviewing for a new position while holding down a current job is tricky. There are only so many "doctor's appointment" excuses you can use before your manager starts to think that you're suffering from some terminal illness. Once you're unemployed, however, you can probably spare some of your suntanning-by-the-pool days for interviews without the lifeguard getting suspicious.

This is all predicated on being able to afford to take time off. Even if you're not too picky, it could easily take six weeks or more to land and start a new job. If you can't afford to take at least three months off without breaking the bank, you probably do not want the pressure of unemployment.

Going Back to School

Whether we long for the days of beer pong or for the (potentially less memorable) intellectual stimulation, many of us dream of going back to school. The grueling schedule of three hours of class four or five days per week no longer seems so bad after years of 40- or 50-hour workweeks. What's harder to stomach, however, is the cost: $40k of tuition for a typical private university, plus another $100k perhaps in lost salary.

Still, it tempts us. Maybe we can switch careers. Maybe we can move up in our current career. Maybe it'll give us the credibility that we need. Maybe, maybe, maybe.

The choice is complex because we never know exactly what we'll gain or give up by going back to school.

The True Cost of Graduate School

Costs for graduate school range widely, but the important thing to remember is that your tuition is only a fraction of the true cost.

- **Tuition.** Tuition varies based on whether a school is public or private; if public, whether you are in state or out of state; and what the field of study is. A typical private institution will cost around $40k, with tuition, books, and other fees. Tuition at a public school for an in-state student might be as low as $10k.
- **Lost salary.** Every year that you're in grad school is salary that you could be getting but aren't. Depending on your previous job and the length of your graduate program, that might be $200k or more. This is usually the biggest factor of the costs.
- **Lost promotions.** In addition to lost salary while you were getting your master's degree, you also lost two years of experience. That's two years of lost promotions and lost raises.

By this math, the one additional year I spent getting my master's degree cost me about $150k. I highly doubt that I got an equivalent bump in earning potential.

Academic Graduate Degrees

Career graduate programs offer you the ability to either switch into a new field, or to obtain a specialty in your existing field. They are often intensely academic programs, where students are often expected to juggle multiple graduate courses while doing additional research.

As rigorous as these programs can be, they can offer you a leg up on your (future) coworkers. You're no longer just any other entry-level employee; you have a specialty. You have unique knowledge that you can offer that relatively few people can compete with. That knowledge can offer the ability to contribute in a way that other people cannot, and to therefore get ahead faster.

The flip side of this is that you may not *want* this specialty anymore once you've invested two or more years studying in it. In fact, this is exactly what many PhDs find; after five to eight years researching a tiny aspect of their field, the last thing they want to do is work in that one, narrow aspect.

Before enrolling in your master's or PhD program, ask yourself:

- **Do you want to work in this field afterward?** If you don't plan on directly using the knowledge from your graduate studies, it may not be worth it.
- **Is the pay worth it?** Look up your desired postschool jobs. How much do they pay? Is the cost of graduate studies compensated for by your expected salary?
- **Are there other ways you can get this experience?** If all you want is some additional knowledge in a field, there may be more affordable and efficient ways to get it. You could, for example, just enter at a lower level and hope to move up.

Preparing Now

The exact ways to position yourself for acceptance will differ based on which graduate program you are enrolling in. If you're applying to a computer science program with only an electrical engineering degree, you may need to refocus your professional work on coding or enroll in additional courses. Other people may already have the "right" background and can get accepted whenever they apply. Regardless, analyze the four areas below:

1. **Academics.** If you're still in college, focus on keeping your grades high. If you have already graduated but have low grades, you might want to consider taking some classes part time at your local university and really, really focusing

on getting good grades. This will help show that you can, indeed, perform well academically.

2. **Professional.** The more closely your professional experience matches your graduate field, the better you'll be. Seek out graduate students in your field and talk to them about what they did before.

3. **Extracurriculars.** Extracurriculars can be a great way to set yourself apart and prove that you're exceptional. Some activities will carry more weight than others, so check with students and professors about what might boost your chances.

4. **Graduate Record Examinations (GREs).** A great GRE score may not ensure your admission, but a poor one can certainly make it much harder to get admitted. Get books, take prep classes, whatever you need to do to ensure that you're in the expected range for the schools you want to go to.

The MBA

Though the cost of a Master of Business Administration (MBA) is quite similar to other graduate programs, the benefits and goals are radically different. For starters, the MBA is a *professional* degree program. You don't enroll in an MBA because you really want to study a specific dialect of marketing; that's what PhDs in marketing are for. You're not studying for an MBA because you love school; if you tell the admissions officers that, it's a pretty good way to ensure your rejection. An MBA is a career move.

For almost as long as MBAs have been around, people have debated whether it's worth it. Not surprisingly, people with MBAs say that it definitely pays off; those without say you don't need it.

The truth is that it depends. It depends on you, your goals, your background, your MBA program, and, well, dumb luck.

However, what you will potentially get out of an MBA is the following:

- **Education.** You will learn a bit about every aspect of business, including marketing, management, finance, and accounting. Understanding each of these areas even at a cursory level can make you more ready to lead a business or business unit. Additionally, during the course of an MBA, you study a broad spectrum of companies, and you begin to develop patterns of analyzing business issues.

- **Experiences.** MBAs are filled with opportunities to lead clubs, conferences, or trips. After all, MBAs are about training the future leaders; it's no wonder they have lots of leadership opportunities. You will also have the chance to attend talks from business leaders around the world.

- **Credibility.** There are certainly those who don't believe in the value of an MBA, but for most people, an MBA from Harvard, Stanford, Wharton (University of Pennsylvania), Sloan (MIT), or Kellogg (Northwestern University) means something. If you previously have an engineering background (as many MBAs do), an MBA will show that you're more than just the typical engineer.

- **Network.** Your classmates will have similar career goals as you (to be really successful in business), but will spread out across fields, industries, and countries. That gives you a broad network of experienced professionals. Need to talk to someone in a senior position in consumer products? Done. Your network is more than just the people you meet; you can also reach out to the full alumni network. When you share this alumni connection, people are much more willing to pick up the phone.

What's in a Name?

Of course, not all MBAs are created equal. You may be able to get a great education anywhere (including for free from books), but the strength of the experiences, credibility, and network will vary based on the school. If you have a Harvard undergraduate degree, go to work for Microsoft and move up to a program manager lead, and then attend Peabody University for your MBA, you probably won't get as much out of your MBA. Your classmates are likely to be much less impressive than you, the alumni network will be weaker, and you'll get much less credibility from this MBA.

That's not to say that Peabody University's MBA is worthless— not at all. It's just probably not valuable enough to compensate for your time and money. Your MBA program needs to be on roughly the same "prestige" level as your prior experience.

Preparing Now

MBA programs want people who will be leaders and will make an impact on the world. You need to have shown that you already *are* a leader, whether it's through starting your own company or through leading projects at work. They want people who have shown success in the following areas:

- **Academics.** Your undergraduate grades are a predictor of your graduate grades, as well as your work ethic and intelligence. You don't have to get straight As, but it'll certainly help if you do. Extremely poor grades can be a deal breaker without something major to compensate for this. If your grades are low, you will need to take extra care that you perform well on the Graduate Management Admission Test (GMAT).
- **Professional.** Find ways to demonstrate leadership in your professional work. If you're a software engineer, MBA programs won't care about the fancy algorithm you wrote; they will, however, care about the projects you led and the

challenges you faced. Working for a big name company also goes a long way.

- **Extracurriculars.** Unless you have an extremely demanding job, top MBA programs will expect that you have gotten involved outside of work, and preferably at a leadership level. Handing out soup in the soup kitchen won't count for much, but being the president of a major help-the-homeless group will.

- **GMAT.** Business school's standardized test, called the GMAT, is a test of your grammatical, analytical, and mathematical ability. You don't need to get a perfect 800 on the test, even for admission to Harvard, but a score below 650 may hurt you. Schools publish their 25 percent to 75 percent range, so make sure you don't fall below that.

The earlier you can plan for this, the better. Many candidates started planning their business school applications two years in advance.

Your "Story"

In addition to proving yourself in multiple areas, your experiences must fit into a coherent story about why you want an MBA, what you'll get out of it, and what your short-term and long-term goals are. As an example, my story was as follows:

My goal is to be an entrepreneur in the technology space. I have previously worked as an engineer for Microsoft, Google, and Apple, which gave me a very strong background in software engineering and gave me the "technical" credibility. I have started two businesses and worked as a start-up, which has given me a taste of start-up life, as well as a picture into the challenges that start-ups face. I am confident that the background in marketing, finance, accounting, and management that I would get as an MBA student at [Your University] would make me a better entrepreneur. I hope to get actively involved in the entrepreneurship club, and expect to start a business either during or directly after school.

An alternative story for a similar candidate might be:

I am passionate about technology, and hope to become a VP or CEO at a major technology company in the consumer products space. I have previously worked as a program manager at Microsoft, where I have had the opportunity to lead the development of several features. I maintain a blog about the newest gadgets, which has offered me the ability to share my insights and receive feedback on them. I hope to double major in marketing and strategy at your MBA program, which will help me to better understand the direction of a company. After graduation, I plan to join Bain, BCG, or McKinsey as a consultant, where I will get to see a wide variety of business problems in a short amount of time. I will then join a medium-sized tech company and work up to a VP or CEO role.

Many of my classmates at Wharton's MBA program admit that their short-term and long-term goals might not have been completely accurate. MBA programs want to know that you understand exactly what you want to want to do in life, and that has encouraged some people to fib a bit with their goals. The best stories, however, tend to be the truest ones.

Part-Time Schooling

The idea of part-time graduate programs is enticing to many. Rather than scrimping to get by for two years while paying tuition and forgoing salary, you get to keep your current salary while "just" taking a few classes on the side. This is a great option for many, but you should make sure that you know what you're getting into.

- **It's really, really hard.** You know how stressed out you get about work? Double it. Your professors won't care that you have a major project due at work; it's not their business. You still need to get all your homework and tests done.
- **There goes your social life.** Many people find that after juggling work and school, they have little time and energy left for friends. You might be able to make it out on the weekends, but grabbing dinner with friends any night of the week is probably shot.
- **You lose some of the value (MBAs).** A core value of the MBA is the network. If you're working full time, you're less likely to get to know your classmates. And to make matters worse, the full-time MBAs may not see you as their peer.
- **You significantly restrict your options.** If you're attending school part time, you are probably not relocating. That means that you are restricted to schools in your area that allow part-time students. Rather than attending the very best school that you can get into, you are restricting yourself to a small set of schools.
- **It's much longer.** Rather than getting graduate school over in one fell swoop, you will likely drag it out over four or more years. Are you prepared to deal with the time, stress, and cost of a graduate program for this long?

On the bright side, you'll have your salary to live off of, and your company may even help pay for your tuition.

Your Questions Answered

Shakespeare Can Write

Dear Gayle,

    I started off college as a computer science major, but switched to English halfway through my sophomore year. My professors were bad, my classmates were antisocial, and the workload was way too much.

    Now that I'm graduating—surprise, surprise—I'm finding that the job prospects for developers are substantially better than they are for writers.

    I think I stand a chance at relearning the fundamentals enough to pass a round of Microsoft-esque interviews. But will they even consider me without a computer science major?

~J. N.

Dear J. N.,

    They might—with enough preparation; but the better question is: are you sure you want that? Remember you dropped out of computer science for a reason and switched to a *very* different major. That's a pretty good sign that the programming life isn't right for you. Plus, it sounds like your primary motivation is money, and that motivation tends not to lead to the best coders.

    Instead, you might consider career paths in the technology space that make better use of your dual interests. You'd be an excellent fit for technical writer, but a career path as a program manager may also be a nice match. There are a lot of options, in fact, for people who understand technology but can also write well.

~Gayle

In Name Only

Dear Gayle,

My company recently had a round of layoffs, which included my own manager. His manager is now the direct manager of my teammates and me, and I've had to step up to take on most of my old manager's work. I'm now effectively the manager of the team, though without the title or the hire/fire responsibilities. I feel like I deserve a raise, if not a promotion. How do I convince the company?

~M. K.

Dear M. K.,

You may deserve a raise, but it's not going to happen. Your company is going through some hard times and can't afford to give you a raise.

Instead, you should see this as an opportunity to get a lot more responsibility than you otherwise would have gotten. You get to acquire a bunch of new skills and prove that you have what it takes to truly fill your manager's responsibilities. Focus on that—learning things and demonstrating your worth.

When the purse strings loosen again, you'll be able to make a strong case for a raise. You can cite the prior

(continued)

(continued)

additional responsibilities as evidence while noting that the company can now afford to compensate you more fairly for your performance.

If the company refuses, then this is an excellent sign to you to begin looking for other options. You're still in a better position than you were prelayoffs because your résumé is that much more impressive.

~Gayle

Newbie Wants Out

Dear Gayle,

I've been working at my new job for only five weeks, and I can already tell I want out. The company told me that I'd be working with customers, other departments, etc., and that's just not true. At best, I work with people who work with customers. Moreover, the culture is just stifling. They say the hours are flexible, but people judge you if you're not there by 9 AM. This is just not the place for me. Is it too soon to leave?

~B. T.

Dear B. T.,

Yes, leaving after five weeks will look bad. I'm not sure you have many other options, though. It doesn't sound like you want to stick it out for a year (the minimum length of time), and making it three or four months isn't much better. It's best to just bite the bullet and leave.

The question is: do you find a job while working or go ahead and quit? All else being equal, the more you can focus on the job search, the better.

There are strategies to minimize the damage to your career and your reputation.

If you can afford being asked to leave immediately, it's best to sit down with your manager and explain the situation: the company isn't the right fit for you, and you're going to start looking for a new position. You'd like to help the company make the soonest transition possible, so you wanted to tell your manager earlier rather than later. This will be an uncomfortable conversation, but it's one you'll have eventually anyway.

As far as what to tell prospective employers, the best answer is the (softened) truth: that the position was very different than you were led to believe, and you decided that it's best just to move on immediately rather than drag things out.

If there's less than about a six-month gap, you don't need to list this short-lived position on your résumé at all. You only need to explain the situation if asked.

~Gayle

Chapter 13

Final Thoughts

Luck, Determination, and What You Can Do

I used to be a big believer in the importance of luck and felt that much of life is up to chance. What would I have been if I weren't born into a family that pushed education—and technology? If I hadn't been raised with the expectation of having a successful, ambitious career? Or if I hadn't been born in a country and at a time where these opportunities are available? No doubt these are some of the greatest strokes of luck that I—or any of us—have had.

As we pass through grade school, then high school, then university, and out into the job market, our luck becomes a bit more controllable. Yes, the people we meet shift our goals and open us up to new opportunities, but we are also in charge of these meetings. How do we connect with people and build on these chance encounters? How do we ask for help or give help to others? How do we develop the skills and resources, so that when we have an opportunity, we can vigorously pursue it?

This book was intended to teach you all those things. You have hopefully learned what skills you need and how to prepare academically and professionally for a career. You now know how to get noticed by a tech company and what elements of a résumé will make them pick it up—or put it down. You understand that you shouldn't just wing it in an interview, that you should even prepare for questions on the topic you know the most about: yourself. You know how to handle the unfortunate rejection, and how to negotiate when you finally get your dream job. And you have learned how to perform more effectively on the job, so that your career can reach the next step. None of these things will make you a luckier person, but they will help take better advantage of your opportunities.

Before you continue your progression through the hiring and career planning process, I would like to leave you with some final advice.

1. **Understand what you have.** You have certain advantages in life, whether that's a degree from MIT or the ability to quickly build relationships with people. These are your strengths. Leverage them to help you reach the next step.

2. **Know what you're missing.** Reading through this book should illustrate what you need to navigate your desired career path, and you should now have a better understanding of what you're missing. If your technical background is weak, take a class. If you have been locked in your cube every day, join a sports team or a volunteer group to meet people. Even the most cursory attempt to cover up your weaknesses will go a long way.

3. **Plan ahead.** While last-minute preparation can be useful, you'll do best with weeks, months, or years of preparation. Years ahead of your desired career step, you need to start thinking about your general path: What do you want to do? And what skills do you need to have? Months before your interview, you create your résumé and connect with people at your target companies. In weeks prior, you prepare for your interviews with preparation grids, practice questions, and mock interviews. And the day before, you rest easy knowing that all your hours of preparation will be worth it. You are on your way to landing a job at one of the world's greatest tech companies.

Good luck!
~ Gayle Laakmann
Founder/CEO, CareerCup.com.

Appendix A

156 Action Words to Make Your Résumé Jump

Sometimes, it's all in the way you say it. Using strong, action words can give your résumé a bit more "oomph!"

The following list will get you started.

Clerical or Detail Work

Approved	Purchased
Catalogued	Recorded
Classified	Reorganized
Compiled	Retrieved
Dispatched	Screened
Implemented	Specified
Monitored	Tabulated
Prepared	Validated
Processed	

Communication Skills

Addressed
Arbitrated
Arranged
Authored
Corresponded
Drafted
Edited
Enlisted
Formulated
Influenced
Interpreted
Lectured
Moderated
Motivated
Negotiated
Persuaded
Presented
Promoted
Publicized
Recruited
Translated
Wrote

Creative Skills

Acted
Concentrated
Conceived
Created
Established
Fashioned
Founded
Generated
Illustrated
Instituted
Integrated
Introduced
Invented
Originated
Performed
Revitalized
Shaped

Financial Skills

Administered
Allocated
Analyzed
Appraised
Audited
Balanced
Calculated
Computed
Forecast
Managed
Marketed
Projected
Researched

Helping Skills

Assessed

Assisted

Counseled

Demonstrated

Diagnosed

Educated

Expedited

Facilitated

Familiarized

Fixed

Partnered

Referred

Rehabilitated

Represented

Management Skills

Assigned

Attained

Chaired

Contracted

Consolidated

Coordinated

Delegated

Developed

Directed

Enhanced

Evaluated

Executed

Forced

Improved

Increased

Led

Organized

Oversaw

Planned

Prioritized

Produced

Recommended

Scheduled

Strengthened

Supervised

Research Skills

Collected

Critiqued

Determined

Evaluated

Examined

Extracted

Inspected

Interviewed

Investigated

Reviewed

Summarized

Surveyed

Systematized

Teaching Skills

Adapted

Advised

Clarified

Coached

Communicated

Enabled

Encouraged

Explained

Guided

Informed

Instructed

Stimulated

Technical Skills

Architected

Assembled

Built

Coded

Designed

Developed

Devised

Engineered

Fabricated

Initiated

Maintained

Operated

Overhauled

Programmed

Redesigned

Reduced

Remodeled

Repaired

Solved

Trained

Upgraded

Utilized

Appendix B

Answers to Behavioral Interview Questions

There may be no "right" answer to behavioral interview questions, but there certainly are a lot of wrong answers. In this section, we'll give example responses (or discussions) for five common behavioral questions and highlight what makes these strong responses.

1. **Tell me about a time when you gave a presentation to a group of people who disagreed with you.**

    "In my last team, I became concerned with a decision the team was making on how to extend our small-business accounting software to personal users. My team thought that we should just create a slightly tweaked version, and I disagreed. I thought we should build a brand new piece of software, and I presented this proposal to the team.

    Most of the work I did to smooth over this presentation was actually before the presentation. I spoke with each of

265

the key decision holders—namely, my manager, the tech lead, and a VP—prior to the meeting. I talked with them about why they felt we should do one thing versus another, and then gathered additional data based on their responses.

Then, in the presentation, I presented the new data and focused the conversation not on convincing them, but rather on understanding what would need to happen for us to make a different decision. We had a very fruitful decision as a team, rather than anyone feeling like we were fighting. We were able to set guidelines to guide our decisions. When we reconvened the next week, I was able to show that we could hit the targets they needed, and that we should reverse our decision. The decision was taken to senior management, who ended up agreeing with the new proposal. We saved our company about three million dollars."

This candidate has shown herself to be analytical, data driven, and collaborative. She made a point of showing how she sought feedback from her team, while still effectively asserting her opinions. She shows herself to be a good teammate and leader.

While this story has a "happy ending," this is not strictly necessary for an effective response. A candidate could, instead, give a humble answer about how she made a mistake in the presentation, and what she learned from it. In fact, the next response is about just this.

2. **Tell me about the biggest mistake you made on a past project.**

"The biggest mistake I made was when I filled in for our tech lead. She had just left for maternity leave, and I was responsible for developing a new schedule to get us to the next milestone. I was embarrassingly off in my estimate.

Here's what had happened. I really wanted to do a good job (I knew this was essentially a trial for a full-time tech lead position), so I solicited input from everyone on the team about the schedule. Each person gave me their estimates, and I compiled these into a greater picture of when we'd do what. I showed it to everyone; they all thought it made sense. And management was impressed that Milestone 3 would be finished in just three months, when Milestone 2 took six. In retrospect, that should have been my first clue.

We ended up finishing after five months, but only after cutting several features. We had agreements with some external suppliers, and we just couldn't let it slip anymore.

I did a few things wrong here that I corrected when I created the Milestone 4 schedule.

First, I didn't factor in risk and all the dependencies. Even if everyone gives a great estimate, things go wrong and you need wiggle room.

Second, I didn't realize that just as I'm trying to impress people as a new (even if temporary) tech lead, everyone else is also trying to impress me. They wanted to show me that they were A+ candidates and gave overly optimistic estimates.

Third, I should have done more to discover the potential risks. Rather than asking, 'Does this look OK?,' I needed to ask people, 'What's the weakness here? What do you think is the most likely thing to go wrong?'

I corrected these things for Milestone 4, added in some comfortable padding, and we ended up coming in just ahead of schedule."

In this response, the candidate has been open and honest and admitted a genuine mistake. Many candidates give responses here about how they "took on too much at once" or "didn't ask for help early enough." While these may indeed be large mistakes, they're also very stereotypical and don't reveal that you can admit your faults.

Remember that this response is as much about learning about your mistakes as it is about understanding if you can be honest.

3. **Tell me about a time when you had to deal with a teammate who was underperforming.**

"In this case, I was actually assigned to mentor the teammate. Vivek had transferred to our team from another division where, to the best of our knowledge, he was doing pretty well. The work was fairly similar, so we expected he would fit in well.

By his fourth week, we realized something was wrong and I was asked to mentor him. Most candidates have submitted at least a bit of code by then, but he hadn't submitted a thing. Every time I asked him about his progress, he said he was doing fine and was 'almost done.' I suspect that he was struggling in multiple areas and didn't want to expose himself by asking too many questions.

Partially based on his prior (rumored) performance, and partially because I just wanted to give him a second chance, I tried a different approach.

I pulled him off his current task (which should have taken him only a few days anyway) and put him on a new and pretty different project—one that he and I would be working side by side on. This allowed him to start fresh, and not have to feel stupid asking questions. It also allowed me to walk him through the project (outlining steps, etc.) without his feeling like I was micromanaging him.

He was able to get through the project with some help from me, but more importantly, I was able to understand exactly what he was struggling with. It turns out that, while he was smart and generally capable, he had some pretty substantial gaps in his knowledge that we needed to deal with.

For some topics, I ordered some additional books for him and taught him some of these areas myself. For others, which I felt the team could use a refresher course on, I had the whole team go through it.

He improved dramatically, and all without having to hurt his ego too much. Within three months, he was performing at expectations, and after another year, he was actually mentoring new hires himself."

The candidate has shown an awareness of other people and has demonstrated that she's a positive person who believes in others. She has proven that she is willing to get her hands dirty; she sat down and worked with Vivek side by side, and then taught him much of what he needed to know.

4. **Tell me about a time when you had to make a controversial decision.**

"I was responsible for engineering at a start-up when the economy tanked, and it became clear that we were not going to be able to raise more money for a long time. We had enough cash left to pay the six current developers for another two years—if we didn't hire anyone else. Unfortunately, we had just extended an offer to one more developer (whom we did really need), and had told another developer that he'd be promoted to a management role when that happened. It was 100 percent my decision how to handle this situation.

Rather than pushing out what was sure to be unwelcomed news, I took the honest and open approach. I brought all the current developers into the room and told them what our cash outlook was. We discussed options as a team, but I asked them to not advocate any specific decisions at this point. I would talk to them all independently.

Everyone was able to see what was pretty obvious—that we couldn't afford additional people—but they felt good about the decision because they helped make it. It wasn't like their big bad manager was telling them that they wouldn't get the promotion or additional help that they needed.

Additionally, one developer took the opportunity to come clean with me. He had been considering striking out on his own for a while and thought this would be a good time to leave. He encouraged us to replace him with the new candidate. He would help train the new employee and field questions after he left.

The honesty and openness that I had shown with my employees made them much more welcoming of the changes and encouraged them to be open with me."

This candidate has revealed an important part of the way he deals with controversial decisions: full disclosure. Alternatively, other candidates might show that they build support around decisions before announcing them, or that they gather data to reconfirm the decision. Whatever your answer is, it will reveal how you solve problems.

5. **Tell me about a time when you had to use emotional intelligence to lead.**

"As a program manager, I am responsible for not only gathering requirements and planning a project, but also assigning who does what. My company is large and generally believes in its rigid hierarchies and levels of superiority. The oldest (tenure-wise, not age-wise) people get to pick what they want to do, and so on from there. The problem is that the younger employees get stuck with menial tasks, resulting in high turnover. I wanted to do away with this system, and I knew that I'd meet a lot of friction along the way.

The first thing I did was just observe. For the first project, I did it their way. This gave me a chance to see the good and bad things, and get to know the people. As much I objected to their system, I didn't want to mess around with something I didn't understand.

The second thing I did was understand what the younger employees wanted to do. Some valued learning, while some valued visibility. Without making any promises to them about the future—I didn't want to get myself into trouble—I asked them to envision what things they'd want to do when they 'one day' have this ability.

Then, third, I went and talked to the senior people expressing, on behalf of the junior people, their desire to have additional learning/visibility opportunities. I asked them to do me a 'huge favor' and stressed that it was totally up to them: I asked them to let the younger people try out some bigger tasks but be mentored by the senior people. This allowed everyone to have a 'stake' in the important projects. Most people were happy to do this.

After this project was done, people were reasonably receptive to switching to this system full time. I realized that most of this issue is really about the ego, and as long as I respected people's seniorities (hence the 'mentorship'), they were pretty happy to work on some less important projects. So far at least, turnover has seemed to drop."

This candidate has demonstrated with this response an ability to understand people. He accurately saw the problems, understood the real driver (ego), and created a plan. He acted carefully and methodically, always making sure he really sees the full pictures. He's the kind of manager people want.

Index